Additional praise for *The One Truth*

"Jon Gordon is the GOAT! He's who guys like me look to and say, 'How is he doing it all?' From his top-rated podcast to his standing ovation speeches to his bestselling books, he walks what he talks in such an inspiring way. Start with this book, but just be warned, you'll want to read everything he writes after you finish it!"

—Jon Acuff, New York Times Bestselling author of *Soundtracks, The Surprising Solution to Overthinking*

"Jon Gordon is passionate about bringing the world together and calls us to *The One Truth* that can make it happen. Whether you are trying to find personal wholesome, or are determined to bring healing to the world, you will find the insights in this book compelling and powerful."

—Erwin Raphael McManus, author of *Mind Shift*, life, mind, and leadership architect and founder of Mosaic

The
One
Truth

ELEVATE YOUR MIND
UNLOCK YOUR POWER
HEAL YOUR SOUL

JON GORDON

Bestselling Author of *The Energy Bus*

WILEY

Published by John Wiley & Sons, Inc., Hoboken, New Jersey.
Published simultaneously in Canada.

For general information on our other products and services or for technical support, please contact our Customer Care Department within the United States at (800) 762-2974, outside the United States at (317) 572-3993 or fax (317) 572-4002.

Wiley also publishes its books in a variety of electronic formats. Some content that appears in print may not be available in electronic formats. For more information about Wiley products, visit our web site at www.wiley.com.

Library of Congress Cataloging-in-Publication Data is Available:

ISBN 9781119757351 (Cloth)
ISBN 9781119757368 (ePub)
ISBN 9781119757375 (ePDF)

Cover Design: Paul McCarthy
Image: © Getty Images / desifoto

SKY10049237_061623

For Kathryn, Jade, and Cole

I love you forever

Contents

BOOK
I

A Higher
State of Mind

Introduction

I remember playing Little League baseball: standing on the mound, throwing a pitch, and hitting a batter with the ball. The next batter walked up to the plate, and I hit him too. I looked over at my dad, who was the manager of the team, and he gave me a dirty look and yelled at me to throw strikes. The next batter got up and the first pitch was out of the strike zone. Then I threw another bad pitch. I looked over at my dad again and I could see the anger and frustration on his face. Each time I looked over he just stared at me and shook his head. I threw the next pitch and hit the batter in the leg. The fourth batter walked to the plate and I could see him shaking as he prepared to get hit with the ball. Everyone watching knew I couldn't find the strike zone and everyone, including him, knew what was coming next. Yes, I hit him too. My dad walked to the mound, replaced me with another pitcher, told me to go play shortstop and finally took me out of my misery. Ever since then I've been searching for ways to be mentally tough.

In eighth grade I told my mom I was depressed and thought about killing myself. She started screaming, "What do you mean you want to kill yourself? Why would you say that?!" She freaked out so much that I somehow snapped out of it to calm her down. I said, "Mom it's okay, I'll be fine," and we never talked about it again. It's probably why, 40 years later, I'm good at suppressing my emotions and why my brother says he "eats his feelings."

In high school, before football and lacrosse games, I would talk to myself during warmups and pump myself up to get ready for the game. I would say things like "You got this. You are going to play great. Go for it. Eye of the tiger." I trained a lot, worked really hard, and always had to earn my starting positions. The coaches never made it easy for me. I often wondered why I always had to prove myself while other players were named the starter without contest. Years later, I realize it made me stronger and grittier, and it taught me what I would need to succeed in college and life.

I was mostly recruited for college football but decided to go to the one school that recruited me for lacrosse, Cornell University. I traveled as a freshman, was a three-year starter, and had a decent college career. Yet I know I could have been so much better. I played with a lot of fear and worried more about making mistakes and getting benched than having fun playing the game. I dealt with a lot of injuries and rarely played healthy. I struggled mentally and physically with the pressure, stress, and demands of being a Division 1 athlete and yet I never gave up. Quitting was not an option. I endured and persevered but would describe my time on the field of play as a job, not joy. I played with a clenched fist, not a smiling face. I wish I could have done it differently but unfortunately no one told me there was a different way.

After college I became an entrepreneur, met my wife, had two kids, and then saw my life and career crumble before my eyes as the company I was involved with crashed during the dot.com bust. I had become more negative, miserable, and fearful than ever and was blaming my wife for why our life was so bad and why I wasn't realizing my dreams. She had enough of my negativity and said that she loved me but she wasn't going to spend her life married to someone who was so miserable and that if I didn't change, it was over. I looked at myself in the mirror and knew a lot had to change, and I began a quest to become a more positive, mentally tough person. She wanted me to go on medication but I told her I wanted to try to do it in a more holistic way.

I began researching the emerging field of positive psychology. I read various studies on gratitude, happiness, meditation, and optimism, and started to put into practice some of these new and exciting ideas. I started taking "thank-you walks," which I'll share later in the book, and practicing self-talk like I did back in high school. I began meditating, which led to walks of prayer, and I created a success journal at night. As I was practicing these ideas and finding much-needed improvements, I began sharing my ideas and practices with others via a weekly e-newsletter, which led to me writing books and speaking. Now, 20 years later, I'm a better husband and father who has helped millions develop a positive mindset and become a positive leader.

I realize now that my entire life has been a quest to get better and to help others get better as well. I've been seeking the keys to improve mental health and become mentally tough. I searched for and shared the tools, habits, and answers for overcoming the fear that wrecks us, the negativity that sabotages our goals, the pressure that rattles our foundation, and the anxiety that limits and weakens us. I've researched and read, learned and taught, trained and developed, written and shared countless ideas in my books to help others win the battle of their mind. As I've become more positive and mentally tough, I've been able to help others do the same. I've had a lot of ideas and answers, but I didn't have *the* answer.

I learned about high state of mind and low state of mind years ago from my friend Garret Kramer, but last summer it became clear that it was part of the One Truth and the answer I had been searching for. As I walked each day and thought about the mind, brain, soul, consciousness, energy, and our everyday experience and reality, I was filled with a greater understanding of how it all works and a practical, powerful way to teach it. I spent the summer teaching it to NFL quarterbacks, NHL general managers, NBA superstars, professional and college coaches, as well as teenagers struggling with anxiety and depression, and they "got it" and reported breakthroughs. I then shared it with several professional and college teams during training camp as well as at several large corporate sales meetings. The response was incredible and like nothing I have ever shared before. I knew I needed to write this book immediately to impact as many people as possible, including you.

I am absolutely convinced that everything in my life has brought me to this moment to share the One Truth with you. The pain, the suffering, the experience on the pitching mound, the struggle with depression, the fear that almost made me crumble, the negativity that almost destroyed me and my marriage, the ideas I've had, the teams I've worked with, the conversations I've had with my friends Garret Kramer, Erwin McManus, Malachi Rhodes, plus the books I've previously written have all prepared me to share this life-changing and next-level teaching and understanding with you right here, right now.

In the pages that follow I'm going to share with you the key to mental toughness, high performance, mental health, and living with power and peace. I know these are bold claims, but I'm confident that once you read and learn what I teach you in this book, it will all make sense, and you will nod your head in agreement. These ideas will resonate deeply with you because they are the truth that already exists inside you. Deep down you already know the truth I'm about to teach you. That's why as you read this book it will feel more like you are remembering than learning as I share examples that confirm what you have thought, felt, and experienced before. You just didn't have words or a framework to explain it. But now you

9

Introduction

do, and I am excited to see how remembering, under-standing, and living the One Truth impacts your mind-set, perspective, and life.

The One Truth and the ultimate way to master your mindset begin with a question I'll answer in Chapter 1.

Chapter 1

States of Mind

Is It the Traffic?

One day you're stuck in traffic and it bothers you; the next day in the same traffic, it doesn't. Is it the traffic making you feel a certain way? If that was the case, it would make you feel the same way all the time and it would make everyone feel the same way. One day you're listening to a song or podcast or just in a great mood and the traffic doesn't faze you. Another day you're pressed for time, have a lot of errands to run, and while sitting in traffic you start screaming. So if it's not the traffic, what is it?

Let's look at other examples to find the answer. A salesperson makes calls every day to acquire new customers and business. One day they receive a rejection from a potential customer and it really bothers them. They feel insecure and start to question themselves, their capability, and their future. Another day, they face the same exact kind of rejection but they move on and make another call with confidence that they will experience success. Is it the rejection that made them feel a certain way?

Consider the pandemic of 2020. Many struggled with their mental health during and after the pandemic, while others thrived. If you read many of the articles about that time, watched the news, and listened to conversations, you would hear people blame the pandemic for causing people to be a certain way, but as we have seen in previous examples, if it was solely the pandemic itself, then everyone would have responded to it the same way. The fact that they didn't tells us there is another reason. To figure this out, let's consider one final example.

Remember in school when you had a paper or project due and you couldn't get started? You were paralyzed by fear or mentally stuck and unable to write or create it. But then you had a burst of clarity and were able to accomplish it. What happened? What changed? Was it the paper or project that caused you to feel a certain way?

It's Always Your State of Mind

The answer is that it's not the circumstance, environment, pandemic, test, project, or event that makes you feel a certain way. It looks like it is but it's not. A closer look reveals it's always your state of mind. If your state of mind is low when the circumstance happens, it affects you a certain way. If your state of mind is high when that circumstance happens, you are able to rise above it, overcome it, and move forward. When you make a mistake on the field, on stage, in a meeting, or on a sales call and you're in a low state of mind, it really bothers you and you start to question yourself and your performance. But if you make the same mistake while you are in a high state of mind, you just brush it off and move forward. You have a next-play, next-moment mindset and look forward to the next opportunity. We've all experienced what it feels like to be in a low state of mind and how great it feels when we are in a high state of mind.

What Characterizes Low and High States of Mind?

A low state of mind is characterized by a lot of thought, a lot of clutter, fear, anxiety, worry, insecurity, and/or doubt. A high state of mind consists of a lot of clarity, focus, belief, and confidence. If you have ever been in the zone or engrossed in the moment of doing something you love without a lot of thinking going on, that is what a high state of mind feels like. And if you have ever felt fearful, with lots of thoughts swirling in your head, making you anxious and tired, then you know what a low state of mind feels like.

Two Circles

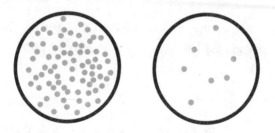

This picture of two circles represents your state of mind. One mind is filled with a lot of thought and clutter while the other has less thought and more clarity. Which mind is at a higher state and which will perform at a higher level? Everyone I have ever shown this to and asked these questions gives the same answer. The circle on the right. The mind with less thought and more clarity is the higher state of mind. We all intuitively know the truth and know the answer.

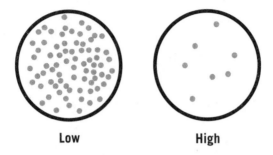

| Low | High |

At this point, like most people, you are likely having a lot of thoughts about this picture and wondering how to have less clutter in order to move from a low state of mind to a high state of mind, or how to maintain a high state of mind when it is high. I promise I'm going to share the best way to achieve and maintain a high state of mind, but before I do it's essential to understand how thoughts work and what lowers our state of mind.

The Roller Coaster

Imagine you're on a roller coaster and you've never been on one before. You don't know that the roller coaster will go back up. So as you race downhill, you think the roller coaster is going to crash. What would you want to do in that moment if you thought the cart you were in was going to smash into the ground? You would want to jump off and escape. When you are in a low state of mind, you want to jump off and escape. It's why people over-drink, do drugs, play video games, and do all sorts of other things to escape the feeling they have when they are in a low state of mind. As an athlete, you don't want the ball when you're in a low state of mind; you want to escape, so you hope the ball doesn't come your way, or you pass it back to your teammate. As a salesperson you don't want to make the sales call when you're in a low state of mind. As a performing artist, you don't want to be on stage in a low state of mind. As a teenager, you don't want to go to school or even get out of bed when you're in a low state of mind. You want to escape the uncomfortable feelings and you often want to escape the reality of life.

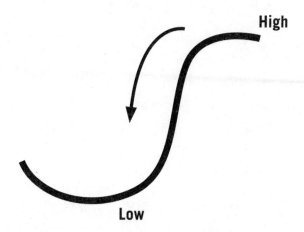

High

Low

Revved-up Thinking

In addition to wanting to escape when you're in a low state of mind, you also can find yourself searching for answers. You have a lot of doubt, and the insecurity can make you think something's wrong. You start searching

States of Mind

for answers to try to fix the feeling that something is broken. This leads to more thinking and more clutter, and thus a lower state of mind.

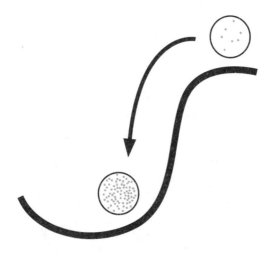

Baseball provides a great analogy. A batter goes 0–4, 0–3, and 0–4 in three straight games. Without a hit in three straight games, they start thinking something is wrong. They examine their swing and wonder if something is broken. The more they think about it, the more they have anxiety. Their revved-up thought increases clutter and lowers their state of mind, causing them to experience a major slump, which leads to more questioning, more thought, more clutter, more frustration, and an even lower state of mind. Does this sound familiar? It happens to all of us in every profession and in everyday life. Think of a guy on a date. He says something that upsets the woman he likes and the date goes horribly. On his next date with another woman he is cautious and anxious and doesn't want to say the wrong thing. He has revved-up thought and a low state of mind. The energy isn't flowing and she declines a second date. Now the guy is questioning everything and feeling even more insecure, which could lead to a downward spiral. So what should you do when this happens to you?

There Is an Ebb and Flow to Thought

Our reality is a world of duality. There is light and dark, good and bad, up and down, love and hate, high and low. As human beings, we experience an ebb and flow of thought, high states of mind and low states of mind. You might even experience different states a few minutes apart, or experience one state for a longer period of time before experiencing another state. You might experience a high state on Friday night and a low state on Sunday night as you think about the week ahead. Your state of mind is like a roller coaster, so you experience an ebb and flow of high and low in the course of your day, week, month, year, and life.

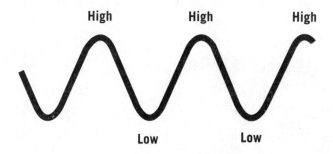

States of Mind

Don't Escape

When you feel like the roller coaster is crashing and you're experiencing a low state, the key is to recognize what's going on and not jump off. Don't try to escape. Realize that being in a low state of mind is normal. It's part of being human. Nothing is wrong and nothing is broken. You are just experiencing the natural ebb and flow of thought. You may feel some discomfort or even pain, but stay in the game. You don't have to fix anything. Stop searching for answers. Stop trying to fix something that isn't broken. The minute you recognize that it's not the circumstance making you feel a certain way, that you're not a victim, and that having a lower state of mind is normal and not a reason to escape, your state of mind rises and you are able to ride the wave back up the roller coaster.

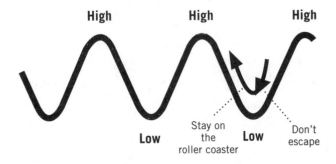

The more you practice this over time, the more you'll find that your roller coaster hills of thought become less steep. The distance between your highs and lows gets smaller. You still have an ebb and flow but the ride becomes calmer and less scary. When you realize the roller coaster of thought is normal and there's nothing wrong with you, you feel a shift immediately in your state of mind. That's because the truth emerges and brings more clarity to you and your life. You now better understand how thoughts work. You aren't the only one who experiences the ebb and flow of thought. Everyone does. It's normal to have a range of thoughts, feelings, and emotions. You are simply human. Too often psychology slaps a label on you and makes you feel like something's wrong with you, which causes you to fix what's broken, which leads to more revved-up thought, more clutter, more anxiety, and feeling even worse. While the intention is good, the result is often bad. In many cases the answer is not to fix what's broken but rather to remember that you are on a path to wholeness, as we will discuss often in this book.

With that said, we've all had moments where it feels like the roller coaster is stuck in a rut at the bottom and there's no way it's going back up. Even when we remind ourselves about wholeness, we may still feel broken. Because of this, I've found that it's very helpful not only to understand the ebb and flow of thought, but also to understand how negative thoughts lower your state of mind and try to keep you down. So before I share other ways to raise your state of mind besides staying on the roller coaster, I want to explain how negative thoughts cause you to spiral downward and lower your state of mind. When you understand the Five D's that sabotage you and your mindset, the answer about how to elevate your state of mind will be even clearer and will make more sense.

Chapter 2

The Five D's

The Battle for Your Mind

There is a battle going on in your mind, and your opponent's weapon of choice is not sticks, stones, bombs or guns but thoughts – thoughts that question your value, purpose, capabilities, goals, future, and worth. These thoughts will often give you doubt; they will weaken you, belittle you, shame you, terrify you, and sabotage you if you let them. They might tell you that you are not good enough, smart enough, attractive enough, powerful enough, or successful enough. They will sometimes tell you the future is hopeless and you should give up. For many, the thoughts try to convince you that the dream you have in your heart is silly and will never be realized. Those dreams are for others, not for someone like you. Negative thoughts might tell you the health diagnosis or the relationship you are in won't improve. They say your past mistakes define you and they try to load you with guilt, condemn you with shame, and imprison you with unworthiness. These thoughts will lie to you during the course of your life and at different times will say that you'll never make it, never be loved, never find the right person, never find the right job, never get through this, and never succeed.

I know these thoughts well because I've experienced all of them and have worked with many people, including some of the greatest athletes and most successful leaders on the planet, who have experienced these thoughts too. For years I lost the battle of my mind because I had

25

The Five D's

no idea I was in a battle. If your enemy knows you're in a battle and you don't know it, you will surely lose. But once you realize you're in a battle and understand how it's being waged, you can create a game plan and strategy to win it. This is what I did in my own life. My mission is to help you win the battle as well.

Your Negative Thoughts Are Not Coming from You

First and foremost, it's essential to understand where your negative thoughts are coming from. So let me ask you: Do your negative thoughts come from you? If you're like most people you'll say yes; "after all, they're in my head." But if you believe your negative thoughts are coming from you, then I have another question for you. Who would ever choose to have a negative thought? Would you choose a thought that sabotaged you and made you feel unworthy, unqualified, and unloved? Would you ever choose a thought that weakened you and ruined your life? Of course you wouldn't. I wouldn't either. I can recall countless times playing sports or speaking on stage when a thought would pop into my head telling me, "Don't mess up! You don't have it today! This could go really bad!" I certainly didn't choose to have thoughts like that pop into my head, and you are not choosing the negative thoughts that pop into your head.

So if negative thoughts are not coming from you, where are they coming from? No one has ever found a thought inside of a brain. I've asked neuroscientists and they agree they have yet to be discovered there. Negative thoughts come from a spiritual place that invades your mind/soul, just like nightmares. When you're having a nightmare, are those thoughts coming from you? Are you choosing these horrible dreams? No, you would never choose a dream like that. It's coming from the field of bad dreams; it's why so many people have similar dreams. There are certain archetypes of dreams, like the one where you are about to take a surprise test that you didn't study for and you panic because you aren't ready. (That's a whole other book.) But the point is that nightmares and negative thoughts are not something you would choose, yet they are always coming in and being downloaded into our brains. Think of it as the internet cloud of software and the brain is the hardware where the activation of the thought happens. Once you understand that these thoughts are not coming from you initially and see how your opponent uses negative thoughts to sabotage you with the Five D's, you will be on your way to winning the battle. So let's talk about the Five D's now.

Doubt

The first D is doubt. This is where negative thoughts begin to break you down. It starts with a thought. "Can you really do this?" "You might fail." "Can you trust God?" "You are going to embarrass yourself and your family if you try this and fail." You'll experience these and hundreds of other forms of doubt that cause you to doubt yourself and everything in your life. You begin to question yourself, lose confidence, and begin to feel weak and powerless. What starts as a seed of doubt grows into a forest of uncertainty, fear, and insecurity.

Distortion

The second D is distortion, which is what happens when the truth is altered. In essence, there is a truth of who you are and the power you possess. Then you have these negative thoughts, which are lies that tell you things about yourself and your future that just aren't true. These lies wreak havoc on you as they accuse you, weaken you, belittle you, doubt you, and do all things I mentioned earlier. It happens very quickly. The thought comes in so fast you think it's from you. Then you believe it, reinforce it, and it becomes an unhealthy part of your soul that eventually discourages you.

Discouragement

The third D is discouragement. This happens when the doubt and distortion (negative thoughts) overpower your mind, seep into your soul, and cause pessimism, apathy, and hopelessness, We don't give up because life is hard. We give up because we get discouraged. We believe the doubt and distortion that we can't win, won't win, and don't deserve to win. We feel defeated, so we stop fighting for what is worthy, noble, and good. If we believe the lie that our negative thoughts are coming from us and we believe the lies that they tell us, we beat ourselves up for being negative and then feel guilt and shame for the thoughts that were never coming from us in the first place. This makes us even more discouraged and lowers our state of mind to the point where we want to escape and jump off the roller coaster.

One of the first people I taught the One Truth to is a teenager who was really struggling. He was so discouraged that, before I talked to him, he had spent a few nights in the ER because of suicidal thoughts. I asked him if he had a lot of negative thoughts in his head. He said that he had so many. I asked him if they were wreaking havoc on him. He said, "Oh yeah, they won't stop. They keep bombarding me. They make me want to just give up." Once I taught him how thoughts work and shared the concept of the Five D's with him, he understood that his negative thoughts were not coming from him and stopped blaming and beating himself up. He also no longer felt guilt and shame. He learned the truth, stopped feeling discouraged, and everything changed. He experienced a complete 180 and was like a different kid. I recently texted him to check how he was doing. He replied, "Doing great, Mr. Gordon. High state of mind." He is one of the reasons why I knew I needed to write this book as soon as possible to reach more people like him. After all, if you don't know how thoughts work, the discouragement can become so heavy and feel so insurmountable that you don't want to keep going. That's why you and everyone you know needs to understand how doubt and distortion can lead to discouragement, which can lead to despair. Despair could be an additional D, but since it doesn't happen to everyone I don't include it as one of the main Five D's, although it's important to mention.

Distraction

Distraction is the fourth D. A distraction is anything that keeps you from what matters most. There's a great saying: "If the devil won't make you bad, he'll make you busy and get you focused on all the things that don't matter, instead of what does matter." You'll look at social media and let the opinions of others define you or compare someone else's life to your own. You'll envy someone's else's mission and forget your own. You'll let social media and the traditional media tell you to be angry at the world instead of working to make the world a better place. You'll spend a lot of time on distractions, being busy but not productive. And over time, you'll realize that distractions are the enemy of greatness and a soul-nourishing life. When you are experiencing doubt and discouragement, this often leads you to searching for answers. But unfortunately, it also leads to you choosing temporary relief and not restoration. Relief is a distraction that masks the pain, but restoration nourishes the soul. I'll share more about restoration later in the book.

Division

The fifth D is division, which is what happens when you experience doubt, believe the distortions, get discouraged, and find yourself distracted. You feel divided. The root of the Greek word for anxiety, μεριζω (merizw), means "to divide, to separate." I believe this appropriately explains why you feel divided when you feel anxious and why you feel anxious when you feel divided. You feel separate from yourself, from others, and spiritually from God. The key understanding here is that negative thoughts cause you to feel distracted, divided, and separate, which leads to a lower state of mind. And it also works the other way. When you feel divided and separate, you experience more negative thoughts. (It becomes a cycle I'll explain more about a few chapters from now.) Negative thoughts divide and cause you to spiral downward. This should all make a lot of sense, since we have seen firsthand how fear – which is a powerful negative thought – divides people, teams, organizations, families, countries, and even the world. Fear separates, weakens, and causes division.

If you let the Five D's beat you, they can lead to a sixth D. Defeat of a team. Divorce in a marriage. And Demise of your life. We see this happen way too often. People who are anxious. Marriages and families divided. Teams dejected and defeated. Politics and the media creating two sides who fight all the time. Countries at war. Our outer world reflects our inner world. If we can win the battle of our mind, we will experience more peace in our own lives and in the world. We don't have to let the negativity win. We now know how the Five D's try to defeat us and we can counter them to achieve victory. The good news is that our plan to win the battle is more practical, purposeful, and powerful. Negativity may seem strong because there is so much of it, but it is no match for the plan and power I'm about to share with you. Instead of letting the Five D's lower your state of mind, now you'll know how to counter them to win the battle and elevate your state of mind.

Chapter 3

Elevate Your State of Mind

Feed the Positive

Over the years I've written a number of books like *The Energy Bus, Positive Dog, Training Camp, Stay Positive, The Power of Positive Leadership*, and others that are all about feeding yourself with positivity in order to feed others. They've had a positive impact on a lot of people, but I must confess that at the time I wasn't sure why they made such a big difference. I knew they helped people become more positive, but I didn't know why positivity makes a huge difference. It's like knowing a car runs really well on high-octane fuel but not knowing why it runs better. What's really happening under the hood and in the engine? Now years later, since understanding how our state of mind works, it makes so much sense. Where negativity lowers our state of mind, positivity elevates our state of mind. Where negativity creates sludge in our pipeline and engine, positivity is a better fuel that flows smoothly. Where negativity brings you down, positivity lifts you up. As I will explain in Book III, the brain is an antenna and you can tune into a positive or negative frequency every moment of every day. When you tune into the positive, it elevates your state of mind.

Tune into Trust

The answer to doubt is trust, and it's only a thought away. When doubt comes in, choose to trust. Trust in yourself. Trust in those you can trust. Trust in the Creator of the universe. Every addiction program believes in a higher power because it's well known that you aren't strong enough on your own. Your will isn't powerful enough. But when you trust and connect with a higher power, you become more powerful than the forces and addictions that can destroy you. As I said, the seeds of doubt will always come in, but you don't have to let them take root in the garden of your mind. Each day you can weed the negative doubts and feed and nourish your garden with positivity and trust. I experience doubt all the time, but when it comes in and I find myself feeling insecure or fearful, I will say a little prayer: "I trust in You, God. I trust in Your plan for my life. I don't have all the answers and I don't know how it's going to work out, but I know You do and I trust in You." It's as if I turn on a light in the darkness and immediately feel a shift in my spirit. I see more clearly and am able to take on the challenge and the day. Where doubt divides you and weakens you, trust connects you to a greater power that strengthens you. Let your trust be greater than your doubt and over time you'll become a powerful force in the world.

Speak Truth to the Lies

Just because you have a thought doesn't mean you have to believe it, especially when negative thoughts are lies that distort the truth in order to discourage and divide you. The key to winning the battle of your mind is to see negative thoughts for what they are – lies – and you'll neutralize them when you stop believing them and speak truth to them. You don't choose the initial negative thought that comes in but you have the power of the second thought in how you respond to your negative thoughts. The best advice I've ever heard is from Dr. James Gills, the only person on the planet to complete six double Ironman Triathlons. (A double Ironman is when you do an Ironman Triathlon and 24 hours later you do another one.) The last time he did it he was 59 years old. When asked how he did it, he explained, "I've learned to talk to myself, instead of listen to myself. If I listen to myself, I hear all the reasons why I can't finish the race. I'm too tired, too old, and too sore. But if I talk to myself, I can feed myself with the words of encouragement that I need to keep on moving forward." Dr. Gills would memorize and recite Scripture. That's what fueled him.

You can speak truth to the lies in order to neutralize the negativity and energize and encourage yourself as you run the race of life. You can talk to yourself instead of listening to the lies that pop into your head. If you're not sure what to say to yourself, here are few truths I know about you:

You are here for a reason.

You are loved.

There is a plan for your life.

You were never meant to be average.

You have a desire to be great because deep down you know there is greatness within you.

You have these thoughts telling you that you aren't enough, but they aren't true. What is true is that you are more powerful than your circumstances. You are more courageous than your fears. Life is tough but you are tougher.

Appreciate to Elevate

I shared in the introduction how a daily thank-you walk changed my life and now I know it's because when you appreciate, you elevate. You elevate your state of mind, you elevate your mood, you elevate your performance, and you elevate the people around you. Since you can't be stressed and thankful at the same time, when you practice gratitude you counter the stress that drains you. Instead of focusing on what you lack, you appreciate what you have. Instead of feeling small, you are thankful for it all. Instead of a scarcity mindset where you don't feel like you are enough or don't have enough, you develop an abundance mindset. I'm convinced abundance flows into your life when gratitude flows out of your heart. When you feel connected to and thankful for everything, you tap into the greater power that gives you everything you need. Where stress and entitlement cut off the flow of positive energy into your life, gratitude for things big and small connects you to it all. Taking a thank-you walk almost every day for the past 20 years, where I would walk and practice gratitude, has had a huge impact on my state of mind. I would walk around my neighborhood, then take a shower, and by the time I got to my office, the garden of my mind was fertile and ready to take on the day and have great things happen. While you may not be able to walk each morning, I want to encourage you to implement a daily gratitude practice such as a gratitude journal or a thank-you drive while in your car or write a few thank-you texts to friends and team members each morning that will elevate you and your state of mind. When I started these thank-you walks years ago my wife noticed a difference in me and my spirit after a few weeks. I believe you will also feel the difference within you.

Encourage Yourself

It's essential that you speak truth to the lies to encourage yourself daily and prevent discouragement from happening. Discouragement makes you want to give up. Encouragement keeps you going. The word "encourage" means to "put courage into," so when you encourage yourself, you are filling yourself with courage to take on the negativity and challenges in life that can cause discouragement. In our positive leadership training we teach a great way to do this. On the left side of a piece of paper, write down many of the negative thoughts you often have. Everyone is different and we all have different thought patterns. You don't have to share them with anyone; just write them down for you. Then on the right side of the paper, write down the words of encouragement you will speak to yourself when the negative thoughts come in. Any time the negative thought appears, talk to yourself and encourage yourself. This will give you courage and power and will elevate your state of mind. My wife discovered that when negative thoughts bombarded her, she would literally say "Stop," and then start speaking positive words to herself. You can too!

Focus on What Matters Most

The answer to the fourth D, Distraction, is to focus on what matters most. And what does matter most? You and your relationships. You being your best for yourself and others. You becoming all that you are meant to be and helping others along the way. You reaching your full potential. Nourishing your mind, body, spirit, and soul is what matters most. As I mentioned before, distractions can derail you and cause you to seek relief, but what you really want is restoration. You don't have to rely on substances to achieve relief and feel better. You can take quiet walks in nature or listen to an uplifting song or spend time with a loving and supportive friend or sit for ten minutes in solitude and meditate or pray. These not only provide relief but restore you as well.

In my own spiritual journey I spent a lot of time practicing meditation and learning mindfulness, which turned into thank-you walks and eventually walks of gratitude and prayer. When you understand how thoughts work, meditation and mindfulness make a lot of sense. They help you have fewer thoughts, which leads to less clutter and a higher state of mind. For me, meditation helped me experience this and then prayer took my mind and soul to a whole other level. Every book I've ever written was the result of ideas that came to me on my walks of prayer. Even this book was the result of walks over the summer, when more and more of the insights came to me.

Busyness and stress will try to get you to focus on what is urgent instead of what matters. The news will consistently try to inject you with fear and pull at you to turn it on once again, only to feel worse. Social media will constantly tell you to envy the lives of others instead of living and creating your own. Bad influences will try to get you to take a quick hit of fleeting happiness instead of living with joy. Distractions will always be available, but each day you can make the choice to invest in the most valuable investment of all: you! And when you become your best you, you can bring out the best in others. It's a simple choice. You can focus on your distractions, try to escape and seek relief, and lower your state of mind, or you can stay the course and focus on what matters most, feed your soul, and elevate your state of mind.

Unite with Love

If the fifth D is divide and fear is the force that divides us, then what unites us? It is love. Love is the most powerful force in the universe, and more powerful than fear. Love casts out fear. So anytime you start to feel fearful and anxious and divided, if you respond with love, the fear will dissipate, and you will feel united. For this reason, love is the greatest mental toughness strategy and performance technique I share with high performers. If you fear making a mistake, worry about performing poorly, fret that you'll let people down, and stew about what critics say about you, then you aren't going to perform very well. But if you focus on loving what you do and love the moment, love the process, and love competing (for athletes), you will perform at a much higher level.

When I first started teaching these lessons, friends of mine asked if I would talk to their son, who was a minor league hockey player. He had gone six games without scoring a goal, which felt like eternity and a death sentence to a young player striving to make it to the NHL. When I spoke to him he was at his wit's end. He was cluttered, trying to fix something that wasn't broken, searching for answers, feeling tons of fear and anxiety, and ready to jump off the roller coaster. After I taught him how thoughts work, the Five D's and the answer to the Five D's, I asked him what he needed to do. He responded, "It's so simple. I just need to stay on the roller coaster, go out there and love playing hockey again and love competing while I'm playing. I need to stop worrying about the outcome and just love the moment and battle." He did, and he scored a bunch of goals in the next few games and was called up to the NHL, and he scored a goal in each of his first two games. When I saw how he played and responded, I knew this teaching would be helpful to many.

Michael Jordan is considered by many to be the greatest basketball player of all time, and many believe his greatness was the result of fearing failure. However, this can't be the case because fear will never drive you to be great. It's part of the equation and a little fear is a good thing. It will cause you to prepare more in order to be your best and often give you a little edge, but it won't be the main driving force of greatness. Love is what drives grit and drives us to be great. After all, if you don't love it, you'll never be great at it. Love had to be Michael Jordan's driving force, so what did he love? In speaking to his coaches and teammates I'm convinced it was his love of competition. He loved to beat you. He actually loved to destroy you. When he was playing he wasn't worried about missing a shot or making a mistake. He was too engrossed in the battle and the moment thinking about ways to beat you. He's a great example that when you love what you do and are engrossed in the moment, fear will have no power over you and you will be a powerful force.

To be the best in the world at something or to simply be your best, love must be the driving force. When famous opera singer Luciano Pavarotti was asked about his incredible discipline for his craft, he said that everyone thinks it's discipline, but it's devotion. He was so devoted to his craft that it drove his discipline. If you are not devoted and you don't love what you're doing, then discipline is hard. But if you are devoted and love it, then you have a higher state of mind and discipline is much easier.

So why does love work? Why does it drive us to be our best? Why does it help us perform at a higher level? It's because the essence of who we are is love. Love connects us to ourselves, to God, and to everyone and everything in the universe. The key word here is "connect." Love creates connection. The more connected we feel, the less fear and clutter we experience and the more clarity we have. Clarity then breeds confidence. If you have ever been in the zone, you know what it's like to be fearless and have amazing clarity and confidence. Time slows down and you see what's happening and know exactly what to do next. Some think that confidence breeds clarity but it's actually clarity that breeds confidence. The more clarity you have, the more confident you feel. Then your confidence leads to courage. The more confident you are the more you are willing to go for it and be courageous. Love creates connection, which leads to clarity, which breeds confidence, which generates courage.

Connection ⟶ Clarity ⟶ Confidence ⟶ Courage

That's why you're more courageous when you operate from a place of love instead of fear. The painter, sculptor, or music composer is not worried or fearful about the outcome when creating their masterpiece. They are doing it with love and are being courageous as they express themselves and share their creation with the world. I remember when I was writing my book *The Carpenter* I had writer's block for the first time in my life. I was stuck and couldn't write. I was fearful that people were going to say my best books were behind me. People were loving *The Energy Bus* and *Training Camp* and I thought they were going to say that this new book didn't compare. I was fearful of writing a piece of junk. Then one morning I woke up with the thought that love casts out fear and all I had to do was love the process of writing, love the reader as I have done before, and love the principles I was sharing. I focused on love and wrote the book in two and a half weeks, and many say it's my best book. I learned that when you love the process, you will love what the process produces.

Keep reminding yourself that love is more powerful than fear and you are more powerful when love, not fear, is your focus and driving force. I told you I was going to share the ultimate way to have a high state of mind and it is *love*. It's so simple, but I've found the closer we get to truth, the simpler and more powerful the lessons are. Fear tries to make things complicated. It clutters us and causes us to search for answers, and yet the solution is simple and the answer is love. Love the moment. Love the opportunity. Love performing. Love the challenge. Love competing. Love striving to be your best. Love failure because it makes you wiser and better. Love success because of how hard you worked to earn it. Love all of it.

To summarize what we talked about so far: Fear and the Five D's divide and weaken you and lower your state of mind, whereas love, trust, truth, appreciation, encouragement, and positivity unite and strengthen you and elevate your state of mind. Here's a picture to help you put it all together visually.

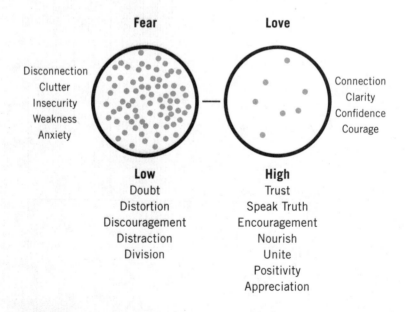

Fear   **Love**

Disconnection
Clutter
Insecurity
Weakness
Anxiety

Connection
Clarity
Confidence
Courage

Low	**High**
Doubt	Trust
Distortion	Speak Truth
Discouragement	Encouragement
Distraction	Nourish
Division	Unite
	Positivity
	Appreciation

Look Inside, Not Outside

When learning to focus on love instead of fear, I find it helpful for people to understand the concept of inside - out to maintain and elevate a high state of mind. When you fear that a certain circumstance has power over you, this lowers your state of mind. But when you know that you and your love are more powerful than your circumstance, this elevates your state of mind. The love inside you is more powerful than the fear of an event happening to you. For years I've been sharing the inside-out message with leaders, sales organizations, sports teams, and schools and have witnessed how this has dramatically enhanced mental health, toughness, and performance.

I remember visiting Clemson University to speak to the football team before their first college playoff game and sharing the inside-out message. I told them it doesn't matter what the media says. It doesn't matter who you are playing. It doesn't matter where you are playing. What matters is that you love competing, love your teammates, and love playing. I said that we always create from the inside out, not the outside in. They got the message, and it has been a part of their mentality and approach ever since. Coach Dabo Swinney consistently reenforces this and tells them "inside out" because he knows how easy it is to forget this truth and to look outside and get cluttered and distracted. It happens to all of us – even me, and I teach this often. It's so easy to look outside at a circumstance and become afraid. Or see a friend have massive success and compare yourself to them and feel inadequate. Or look at your sales quota and sales numbers and become afraid you won't hit them. Or have a series of unfortunate events happen and become fearful. You have to continually remind yourself to look inside, not outside.

I was speaking to the Oklahoma City Thunder basketball team years ago. As I was walking across the court, the coach and a superstar basketball player who were talking stopped to ask me, "Hey Jon, we were just wondering. What has a bigger impact on an opposing team – homefield advantage in baseball or homecourt advantage in basketball?" I paused for a moment and told them it's neither. When you know that the outside is just noise and people yelling, and that you create from the inside out, from your spirit, passion, love, soul, the outside has no power over you. The superstar basketball player said, "That's what I think. It seems like 98% of guys in the league believe in home court advantage but I know it isn't true, so I just go do what I do and play my game. I told him, "That's because you are looking inside, not outside." I want to encourage you to do the same. When the circumstance happens – whether it's a test, traffic, or more serious adversity – remind yourself of what I said in the beginning of the book. It's not the circumstance; it's always your state of mind, and the circumstance has no actual power over you. Your love is more powerful than your fear.

Move from Clutter to Clarity

People often say to me, "Okay, Jon, I get all this, but when I'm in the moment and I lose my focus or feel cluttered, what can I do? What's a key strategy? I believe the key is to remind yourself of these truths and concepts and talk to yourself. Here are a few things you can do; pick what works best for you:

- Remember, it's not your circumstance; it's your state of mind.
- Stay on the roller coaster.
- Talk to yourself and speak truth to the lies.
- Practice gratitude.
- Tune out distractions; focus on what matters most.
- Focus on love, not fear.
- Focus on inside, not outside.
- We create and live from the love inside of us to overcome the fear that is trying to sabotage us.

Power or Powerless

The UCLA women's basketball team was one of the first groups I taught about high state of mind and the One Truth. After I shared the framework with them, I asked them to tell me what happened when one of the top gymnasts in the world chose not to compete in one of the competitions during the Olympics for mental health reasons. One of the players stood up and said, "She felt pressure from all the expectations. She was looking outside at the media, the judgement, and the competition, and felt separate. As a result she had a lot of thoughts, clutter, fear, and anxiety, which led to a low state of mind and her deciding to escape, jump off the roller coaster, and pull out of the competition." This player absolutely nailed it and demonstrated that when you understand this teaching, you'll see clearly how it applies and plays out in our lives.

I told the team that critics who mocked the gymnast for pulling out of the competition and derided the younger generation as soft and mentally weak were completely wrong. I don't think she was being mentally weak at all. I don't think our younger generation is soft. I believe the younger generation is being bombarded with negative thoughts, constantly looking outside via social media (I share more about this in Book II) and believing the lies that are separating and dividing them and attacking their identity and self-worth. So we shouldn't criticize them. We should empower the younger generation with the truth and ideas I share in this book so they possess the strategies and strength to not allow outside forces to affect their mental health. Instead of them feeling like a victim, we can help them realize their true power. I told the UCLA team that the key is to teach everyone the truth, that it's

The One Truth

not the circumstance but rather our state of mind, so that when something like this happens, they will understand what's really going on and tap into their power instead of becoming powerless.

The End or the Beginning

When I speak to businesses, schools, and sports teams about how to have a high state of mind, I usually end my talk and teaching right here. Learning how thoughts work, understanding high and low states of mind, feeding the positive, overcoming negative thoughts and the Five D's, being grateful, speaking truth to the lies, focusing on what matters most, tapping into the power of love to overcome fear, and looking inside instead of outside are all powerful and proven concepts and strategies to improve mental health, mental toughness, and high performance. But I must confess there is a whole other level and truth to this teaching that explains high and low states of mind at a deeper level. This understanding can be viewed through the psychological, consciousness, spiritual, and biblical lenses. If something is the truth, it will be found everywhere, in every teaching and in every understanding. If you are simply happy in knowing how to raise your state of mind, you can stop reading right now. This will be the end of the book for you.

However, if you are someone who wants to go deeper and understand how the One Truth not only influences our state of mind, but explains the unseen forces that weaken us and hidden power that impacts leadership, teamwork, relationships, addictions, social media, anxiety, mental health, thoughts, trauma, healing, and literally everything, this is just the beginning. If you turn to Book II, you'll discover the One Truth, and learn how this truth is applicable to everything in life, and how it determines what we create and experience.

BOOK
II

The One Thing
That Explains
Everything

Chapter 1

The One Truth

Oneness and Separateness

When I taught you about low and high states of mind, I explained how fear divides and negative thoughts separate you, and how love and positivity connect and unite you. Well, the One Truth is that our state of mind, the thoughts we think, the words we say, the life we live, and the power we have and everything we experience are ultimately influenced by oneness and separateness. Think of a team that is divided. They feel separated from each other and are weak. Now think of a team that is united. They are connected, powerful, and strong. The same goes for you. When you feel a sense of oneness, connection, and unity, you feel powerful, confident, and strong. When you feel separate, you feel divided, weak, and powerless. When you feel connected and one, you have a high state of mind. When you feel separate, you have a low state of mind. When you feel oneness, you feel love. You feel like you are home. When you feel separate, you feel fear, like a child who is lost searching for your way back home. When you feel oneness you experience the essence of love. When you feel separate and alone, fear arises and, as I will explain, it leads to every weakness, negative thought, and destructive behavior humans have. Here's a visual that explains how the one truth affects our state of mind.

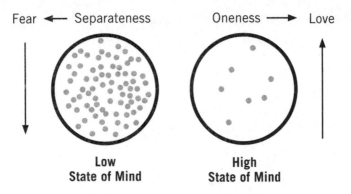

Fear ◄── Separateness   Oneness ──► Love

Low
State of Mind

High
State of Mind

Positive to Negative

The more we move from oneness to separateness, we move from love to fear, from high state to low state, and from positive to negative. Compare a normal mental health condition to mental health disorders; normal to disorder moves from positive to negative. We never say that someone has a mental health issue because they have too many positive thoughts. The most common mental health disorders are associated with feelings of isolation, fear, separation, anxiety, disconnection, and negative thoughts. The person feels separate and their brain functions in a way that experiences this disorder. And the more a person feels separate, the more they separate themself from others. It's why many people with mental health challenges isolate themselves from life and relationships instead of connecting. I'll explain more about how and why I believe this happens, but for now understand that the root cause is oneness and separateness.

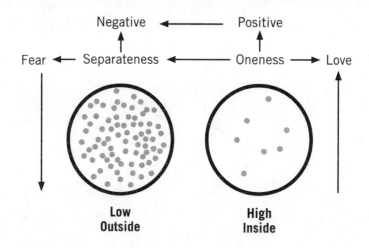

Inside and Outside

In the beginning of the book I explained how it's never the circumstance that makes you feel a certain way but rather it's your state of mind. I also shared the importance of looking inside instead of outside to have a high state of mind. This is because the more you look inside, you see and remember the truth that you are one and not separate. The more you look outside and focus on your circumstances, expectations, comparison, and negativity of others, you forget the truth and believe the lie that you are separate. As I will explain, life and other forces are always driving you to look outside and cause you to feel separate and weaken you. When you believe the lie that you are separate, you feel weak and lose your power. But the more you look inside and remember the truth that you are one, you feel and are powerful.

If you continually felt oneness, you would always feel love and never know fear, insecurity, or doubt. You would live permanently in a high state of mind and a perpetual zone state. But as I said earlier, we live in a world of duality and there are many times you fall for the lie, as do I, and feel separate. And because of this you experience fear, negative thoughts, insecurity, anxiety, and this leads to you searching for relief and a low state of mind, instead of knowing you are one and a high state of mind.

Searching and Questioning vs. Knowing

If you have ever lost your wallet, glasses, phone, or something else important to you, you know the frantic feeling of looking for it. When it's with you and you know where it is you feel good, but when it's lost and you're looking for it you feel very stressed and unsettled. As you move from oneness to separateness and from love to fear, high state to low state, and inside to outside, you will find yourself searching for answers, questioning yourself, and feeling lost. As I mentioned earlier, when you have a low state of mind, you feel like something is broken. When you feel like something is wrong, you spend your time – and in many cases your life – searching for answers and looking for a solution, which leads to revved-up thought and clutter. It also leads you to desire a positive feeling as you search for a sense of love, peace, connection, and oneness, instead of feeling isolated, alone, fearful, anxious, disconnected, and unhappy. Rather than feeling at home, you feel like something is lost.

Because so many people feel separate and don't understand why, they fill the gap with substances that take away the pain, suffering, and discomfort they experience from searching and questioning. This is what leads to addictions. Addicts are seeking love and the feeling of oneness, but fill the gap between oneness and separateness with cheap substitutes that don't fulfill what their soul really longs for. They seek more and more and wind up feeling worse and worse. The search leads to more suffering, the gap between oneness and separateness gets wider, and they go further along the downward spiral. This is why addiction programs that create community and believe in a higher power are effective. As you surrender and connect to others through community and a higher power, you no longer feel alone. You feel less separateness and discomfort and more oneness, love, and acceptance, which begin to restore you.

Chapter 2

The One Truth Applied

A New Lens

To understand the One Truth at a deeper level, it's helpful to see how it applies to our lives at a practical level. Once you see how oneness and separateness, inside to outside, knowing to searching, and positive to negative impacts you, your team, your relationships, and every aspect of your life, you won't be able to unsee it. It will be a new lens for you to see the world and how you and others interact with it. As I share a number of common topics, scenarios, and issues that are part of our everyday life experience through the One Truth lens, my goal is that you'll realize what's happening at a deeper level, within yourself and others, and with this knowledge and understanding you will live more powerfully in this world.

The Narcissist Feels Separate

Psychology considers narcissism a psychological condition called narcissistic personality disorder, which usually arises because of emotional injury and trauma from shame, loss, deprivation, and painful experiences in childhood. Research and brain scans show that the narcissist's brain actually blocks off parts to protect itself based on traumatic experiences and painful memories. The brain literally creates separation and division at the neurological level, which I believe is a manifestation of the separation that a narcissist experiences. At a deeper level the narcissist has moved from oneness to separateness. They feel separate, isolated, and alone so they focus solely on protecting their separate self and only care about themself, not others. They lack empathy and concern for how their words or behavior affect others. It's why narcissists make horrible leaders. As Maya Angelou said, "You can't be much of a leader if all you see is yourself. A leader sees greatness in others."

Not surprisingly, narcissism is also associated with a big, fragile ego that doesn't handle criticism well, constantly seeking praise and admiration from others, and swallowing people's energy like a black hole while also experiencing frequent depression and anxiety. As I will explain later, the more a person feels separate, the more they will struggle with a variety of mental health conditions. When you understand how oneness and separateness affect the brain and thoughts, and how the brain and thoughts interact, it will make a lot of sense. If we can get a narcissist to return to oneness and see themself as part of a bigger whole, they would feel more whole themself. If we can help them heal the trauma of the past and know they are loved, they would be able to heal their soul and brain in the process. Like the soul, the brain heals through connection, and this connection leads to restoration.

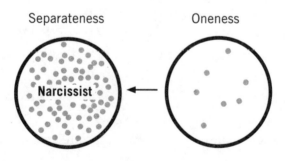

Two Becoming One

A coach and player have a heart to heart, get real and vulnerable with each other about their fears of failure, and become unbreakable and unshakable after the meeting and win a Super Bowl. A teacher and student discuss the student's behavior in class and the student shares that they are going through a tough time at home. The teacher listens with empathy and shares love and support. The student starts to thrive in class and in life. A mental coach talks with a musician and shares advice, but more importantly provides unwavering support and belief in them. The musician takes their performance to a whole new level. A team has a meeting after a series of tough losses and after some initial yelling and screaming, they get vulnerable and share what's holding them back. They turn it around and go on an incredible win streak. A family sits together at a table every Sunday and discusses the challenges each person is facing and they come up with solutions together. Everyone walks away from the table feeling more confident and the family creates a lasting bond. A married couple takes a walk on the beach and talks about some of their issues and after fighting for a little bit they listen and vow to be better for each other.

In all these cases the connection that happens is more important than the advice, solution, and words spoken. What's happening at a deeper level is connection, unity, and oneness. Each person is moving from the feeling of being separate and alone to feeling connected and one with each other. From this oneness, a feeling of love flows and healing and power is experienced that transforms the individual, the relationship, and the team. HeartMath has conducted advanced research and found that when people are experiencing these types of connections there is a synchronization of the two hearts that begin to act as if they are one. We were created for connection. The latest research in relational psychology shows that we heal in connection. The research demonstrates the truth that we were never meant to be alone and separate. We are wired at the spiritual, soul, biological, and cellular level to become one, and when we do we experience greater power, connection, commitment, and healing.

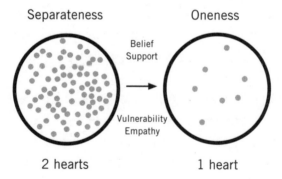

One Couple

Two people meet and begin a relationship and eventually get married. They have issues from their past that they haven't dealt with. The fairytale romance quickly becomes a nightmare as their issues surface and they start fighting a lot. Instead of loving and nurturing each other, they each become defensive and protective of themselves. Instead of being on one team, they feel like they are on two teams. The man grows frustrated, jealous, and bitter. The woman becomes increasingly sad, insecure, and hopeless. They live in the same house and even sleep in the same bed, but they feel alone. The relationship is headed for divorce, but after a big fight the woman suggests they go to counseling. The man reluctantly agrees, and after talking and sharing, their issues come to the surface as they each listen to the pain and hurt the other is feeling. They focus more on loving each other instead of fighting with each other. Instead of feeling insecure they now feel safe, and this draws them closer together. As they address and heal their past issues, they grow individually and together. The closer they become and the more love they share and feel, they both heal and grow through love, connection, and oneness. I know this story well because my wife and I lived it. We heal in a loving relationship. Love and oneness transform us and each other.

One Team

How do you outperform a team that has more talent? Be more connected and committed. A team that becomes One will outperform a group of talented separate individuals. When a team moves from selfish to selfless and "me" to "we," they move from separateness (weakness) to oneness (power). I have worked with countless teams over the years and have helped them become more connected and committed. I've worked with NFL, NBA, MLB, NHL, and college teams that have won championships and whenever they win they talk about the love they have for each other, the sacrifices they make for each other, the selflessness and the commitment. Of course, you have to have a level of talent, great coaching, a strong culture, and alignment at all levels of the organization, but the most important factor of all is oneness. Do they transform from a group of individuals into one united and connected whole team? A team with a group of individuals has a lot of individual weaknesses, but a team that becomes One has a collective strength. It's always the key ingredient because division and separation lead to weakness, whereas oneness brings power, unity, and strength. This is why I share a bunch of team building exercises in *The Power of a Positive Team* that foster connection and unity and dissolve egos and division.

One of my favorite exercises is the Triple H: Hero, Hardship, Highlight. While the team sits together, each person stands up one at a time and shares who their hero is, a hardship they faced that made them who they are today, and a highlight in their life they are proud of. As each person does this, especially the hardship story, you can feel the change in energy in the room. Tears often flow. The walls of pride and ego come crumbling down and vulnerability and authenticity pave the way for connection, love, unity, and oneness. After one session I had with a college golf team, the coach contacted me a week later and said, "I've never seen a group of golfers (who play an individual sport) become more connected than this team has. They are now rooting and cheering for each other. They have become a team." Not surprisingly, they won a championship that year. Oneness is power and as each person feels the oneness within themselves, they become part of the *whole* team, and as each teammate experiences the oneness of the team, they feel more whole and less separate themselves. For years I knew my approach worked but I couldn't explain exactly why; now in understanding the One Truth it all makes sense. Teammates who are part of *one* team feel more connection and love, which gives them power instead of the fear and division that weakens them. This leads to greater clarity, confidence, commitment, and courage and a higher level of performance.

Note that although I share sports examples, the same principles and truth apply to all teams. I've seen the same thing happen with business teams, school staffs, church teams, nonprofit teams, marching bands, and all types of teams I've had the opportunity to work with. The reason why I share sports examples is that it's easy for everyone to see how the principles translate within a season by watching a team perform on the field or court.

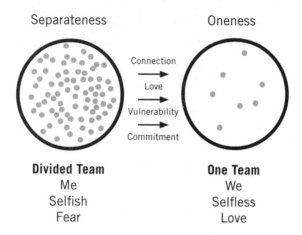

Separateness   Oneness

Connection
→
Love
→
Vulnerability
→
Commitment

Divided Team   **One Team**
Me   We
Selfish   Selfless
Fear   Love

When Low Meets Low

After I shared the One Truth with the Dallas Cowboys coaching staff, they asked how they could help their players have a high state of mind. I said first and foremost, you remember the truth and you have a high state of mind. When you have clarity you can help your team have clarity. If you have a low state of mind and are cluttered, you won't be at your best for your team. The worst-case scenario is when you have a coach with a low state of mind engaged in a heated moment with a player with a low state of mind. It's not a good thing. They laughed, knowing what that moment feels like because we have all been there. Anyone with kids will attest to this. When you are in a low state of mind and your child is in a low state, it often leads to tension, disagreements, and crying – sometimes from both of you. When you and your spouse are both in low states, it leads to fighting and saying things you regret. Stress is often the observable cause, but at a deeper level you both feel separate. You don't feel as one, so you don't act as one. You don't act like you are on one team because you feel like you are on separate teams. When low meets low, a greater separation is often the result.

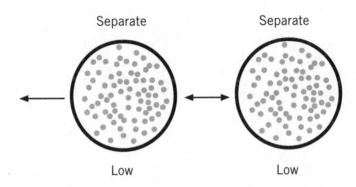

Separate   Separate

Low   Low

Fear of Change

Separateness affects offices and organizations going through change. When change is occurring and communication is poor, uncertainty and fear arise and this leads to low states of mind and a feeling of greater separateness. As a result everyone focuses on themselves and not others. Members of management look out for themselves. Employees each try to protect themselves and as a result engagement plummets, people leave, and those who stay just try to hang on. When you are in a low state and fearful you focus on just trying to survive. You aren't thinking about helping others thrive. Most change initiatives fail not because of the change or initiatives but

73

The One Truth Applied

because of the lack of communication, trust, and leadership that is driving the change. Change management that understands the One Truth and how uncertainty and fear can lead to greater separation and takes steps to create unity and trust will be more successful. I helped the leaders of Dell and EMC become *one team* as they merged to become one company and it led to great connection and collaboration amongst the leadership.

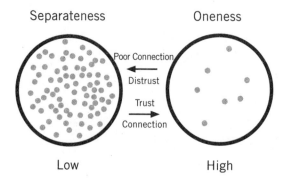

Change

You Are the Traffic

Imagine two people who are in a low state of mind driving in traffic. They both want the same spot on the same road and see themselves as separate from each other. One driver cuts the other driver off. Let's just say the interaction is not very positive and seriously it's how road range incidents happen. The interesting thing is that each driver sees the other as the cause of the traffic. Since they feel separate they see each other as separate and thus the one to blame. But in Los Angeles – home to some of the worst traffic in the United States – a brilliant sign read, "You are the traffic." In essence since we are all one, we are all the traffic. When you realize this truth, you stop seeing others as separate and part of the problem. In fact, the circumstance is not even a problem. The lie that you are separate is the problem. Remember the truth and enjoy the ride.

Pressure Believes the Lie

People often say the pressure got to them or they felt the pressure. Some mental coaches try to train people to believe pressure is a privilege and pressure is your friend. That's a step in the right direction because it's turning a negative into a positive, but it's still not based on the truth. So what really is pressure? It's looking outside and believing that expectations, opinions, criticism, and forces outside you can impact how you feel. But in truth we know that anything outside you can only impact you if you believe the lie that it does. Thus, my definition of **pressure** is *believing the lie that anything outside you can impact how you feel and perform*. When you know the truth that this isn't the case, the lie fades away and so does the pressure. This is what happened to the minor league hockey player I mentioned in Book I. When he got back to playing the game he loved and looked inside instead of outside, the lie and the pressure faded away and he performed at a much higher level. For those who believe the lie, the pressure can feel like a ton of bricks sitting on your chest. No wonder so many want to escape and jump off the roller coaster, as I mentioned in Book I.

Pressure

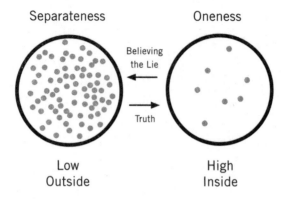

Separateness   Oneness

Believing
the Lie

Truth

Low   High
Outside   Inside

Unworthy and Perfect

I would also add to this that pressure happens when you are fearful and worried that if you don't perform well, then you aren't worthy. When your identity is tied to your performance and how you do defines you, you must do well to think well of yourself or to have others think well of you. If you do poorly, then you think you are worth less. This is all a result of separateness. When you feel separate you have to find a way to be worthy and powerful, so you focus on searching to be something instead of knowing how valuable you are. When you feel unworthy you usually go in one of two different directions. You cither feel separate and powerless and retreat from challenges and life or your separateness leads you to strive to be a perfectionist in order to feel worthy and powerful. Unworthiness and perfectionism are two sides of the same coin. Because you feel unworthy, you strive to be perfect to receive validation and recognition and to become worthy. Perfectionists feel a ton of pressure because they are constantly having to feed the lie that outside praise and success are essential for their self-worth. Every test, job, performance, and project is an indictment of who they are and what they are worth. They live in a state of fear of not being enough, and this leads to constantly working and striving for validation.

I know this well because this is how I played lacrosse in college and lived most of my life until my life came crashing down. Only when I lost everything, and my identity was crushed, did I find the one thing that truly mattered and made me who I am: my connection to God. Looking back, I saw that it was a miserable and exhausting experience to constantly define myself by my accomplishments, opinions of others, and status. When you live this way, you don't feel like you are enough, so nothing you do is ever good enough. It's like you have this big hole that you're always having to fill with a shovel and sand. The more you work and strive to fill it, the bigger the hole gets, and you feel like you always have more work to do. You never feel satisfied, accomplished, or at peace.

Fame and Celebrity

Many seek fame and celebrity for the same reasons others are perfectionists. They feel separate and so they try to fill the hole and separation with fame to feel validated and receive recognition. If others see them, recognize them, and praise them, then they are worthy. They matter because they matter to others. But fame and celebrity are very dangerous because what happens when the lights turn off, the cameras stop following you, the media stops talking about you, and people stop praising you? Who are you then? The hole becomes a canyon and you feel more separate than ever. Narcissism, ego, unworthiness, perfectionism, and fame are all the result of feeling separate, which leads to a hole that you try to fill with things that will never fill it. When you understand the One Truth, you see the madness and dysfunction that result from trying to fill a hole with material that doesn't fill it and actually makes the hole bigger and makes things worse.

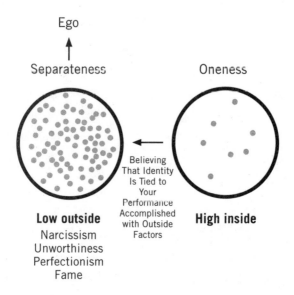

Ego

Separateness   Oneness

Believing
That Identity
Is Tied to
Your
Performance
Low outside   Accomplished   **High inside**
with Outside
Narcissism   Factors
Unworthiness
Perfectionism
Fame

Social Media Is Not the Problem

When you know the One Truth you will see that although people say social media is the cause of what ails our country and is the reason why so many are struggling with their mental health, in fact social media is not the problem. The problem is separation that causes us to look outside and compare ourselves to others and feel unworthy. Social media is simply the vehicle that causes us to constantly look outside and not inside. We've done it for years even when there wasn't social media. We looked outside when we read the papers, watched the news, looked at the tabloids, watched reality TV, were jealous of the cool crowd in high school, or strived to be a part of the in crowd in our community. A generation ago, when you saw that a neighbor got a new car, you might have gotten jealous. Now you see it online. The problem with social media is that it makes it so much easier to look outside and compare more often. When you look outside on social media, you see other people's highlight reels and compare them to your own flaws and failures. As Jerry Flowers Jr. says, they don't have a better life; they just have a better editor. But when you are constantly looking outside with a low state of mind, you often forget the truth and compare, which leads to despair. The more separate you feel, the more you return to social media like a drug, only to feel worse. In looking at social media and feeling increasingly separate, you activate the unworthiness, insecurity, fear, ego, and need for validation that comes from believing the lie that you are separate. Social media then pounds your soul with this lie and it wreaks havoc on your mental health and well-being.

People often say the solution is to get off social media, and while that's not a bad idea for many of us, the real answer is to apply the One Truth and see social media for what it truly is: a vehicle that constantly reinforces the lie that you are separate and causes you to look outside and compare and feel worse about yourself. The answer is to look inside and know you are one and anything you see outside you, including social media, has no power over you. When you remember that you are one and remember your power, you should be able to look through social media and not have it impact you. This is real and true power. If it does bother you, it's a sign letting you know you are feeling separate. In oneness you love others, celebrate others, are happy for others and their lives do not define yours. We always create from the inside out! As I tell teenagers all the time, never let the opinion of others or social media define you. You are defined by so much more, as I'll share in Book III. This is truth.

Social Media

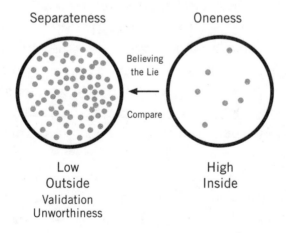

Separateness

Oneness

Believing
the Lie

←

Compare

Low
Outside
Validation
Unworthiness

High
Inside

The One Truth

Racism

I know this is a very sensitive topic to discuss but I believe understanding the root of racism is helpful in curing it. At its very core, racism is the result of looking outside and feeling separate, seeing skin color and/or ethnicity and having a distorted reality that you are not only separate from someone but better than them. Instead, if you look inside within the soul, you see that you share the same humanity and spirit as someone who looks different than you. When you see that you are one, you won't have any connotations of ill will or superiority toward someone. While diversity training helps people to understand, respect, and appreciate differences and uniqueness in others and serves a worthwhile purpose, I believe Oneness training would be even more powerful and impactful. While it's helpful to understand different cultures, races, and ethnicities, the greatest change will happen when we understand and reinforce how we are connected, and share the same spirit and humanity. My friend Miles McPherson, a pastor in San Diego, created and teaches such a program called the Third Option, which seeks to create connection and oneness.

I love the concept of Namaste, a greeting used in yoga that means that the spirit in me recognizes and bows to the same spirit in you. It is the acknowledgment and sense of oneness, connection, and love from one soul/spirit to another. If each one of us would understand and recognize this oneness and connection to their fellow humans on this planet, regardless of how they look, love would reign and racism would cease to exist.

Love and Purpose Flow from Oneness

I was talking to my friend Garret Kramer about my son, who was struggling with finding his purpose in life. I said he needs to start volunteering, serving others, and living with purpose to find his purpose. Garret paused for a second and said, "No, it doesn't work quite that way. Just because you volunteer doesn't mean there's meaning and purpose connected to your actions. You could serve and volunteer and still feel separate. You can be doing something most feel is purposeful and go through the motions and not feel any purpose while doing it. Your son simply needs to remember he is one and when he no longer feels separate, love and purpose will be a byproduct of the oneness and connection he feels.

The minute he said it I saw the truth so clearly. Love and purpose flow from oneness. The more you feel one, the more you want to share more love and help more people. You see pain and suffering, and because you feel whole, you want to help others experience wholeness. Because you feel love, you want to share your love with others. Your actions don't drive your intention. Your intention drives your action. As a speaker, I always remember the words of Luciana Pavarotti. He said everyone wants the audience to love them, but he loved the audience. He may not have known why he loved the audience, but I can tell you it was because he felt one with the audience, not separate from them. It's the same way in life. When you feel separate you want others to validate you, but when you feel one you feel a greater purpose to impact others and love them.

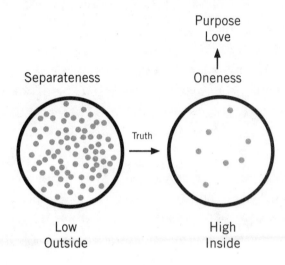

The Leader with Integrity

Integrity is the number-one way to build trust and create success. The word "integrity" comes from the word *integer,* which means whole or complete. A leader with integrity is whole and complete. There's no gap between what they say and do. There's no separation between their character, values, principles, and actions. Their actions are representative of their values and principles. Because of their wholeness and alignment, leaders with integrity earn trust from others and are impactful and powerful leaders, whereas leaders who have an integrity gap and a gap in their character are weak leaders.

Who you are determines how you lead. Leaders who are whole build trust and create lasting success, whereas those who have a gap and separation (such as the narcissist we discussed earlier in this chapter) struggle in their ability to lead and impact. Those who lead with ego and fear in order to gain power might deliver short-term results, but over time their gap, separation, and incongruency will lead to their demise. On the other hand, the leader with integrity who empowers others will gain power and influence. In most cases, leadership and character gaps come from a wound, so it's helpful to know how wounds impact you at a deeper level, keep you from experiencing oneness, and what you can do about it. We'll talk more about that in Book III.

Integrity

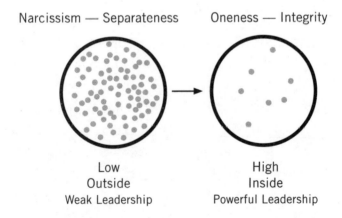

Narcissism — Separateness

Oneness — Integrity

Low
Outside
Weak Leadership

High
Inside
Powerful Leadership

The One Truth

Ego Is Not the Enemy

We often hear the phrase "Ego is the enemy," but actually separation is the enemy. When you feel separate, you feel powerless. This gives rise to the EGO, which is an acronym for Edging God Out. EGO props up and tries to give you a sense of power, but it's actually weak, false power, because it's limited to self and not connected to a higher and greater power. It reinforces the sense of self and bolsters the lie that you are separate, which further disconnects you from the power and oneness you seek. If you are filling yourself up by feeding your own ego, then God can't fill you up. You are full but not fulfilled.

When you have a big ego you act like God because you feel disconnected from God. Because of this disconnection, the ego causes you to fill yourself up in a variety of ways, such as accumulating power and money, seeking a prestigious job title, striving for success, chasing fame, looking for the applause of others, and a variety of ways that feed your *self*. But it's never enough because it doesn't fill you up with the love and connection you truly seek. The more EGO drives you, the more you reinforce the lie of separateness and the more disconnected you become.

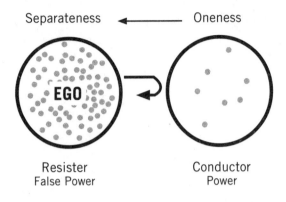

Separateness ← Oneness

EGO

Resister
False Power

Conductor
Power

In the world of electronics, the resistor relies on its own power and holds on to its electrons. As a result, its power is limited. But a conductor freely gives and receives its electrons. It knows that its power comes from the source and power that flow through it. Ego causes you to be a resister, whereas humility allows you to be a conductor. Humility is knowing there is a God who is not you, and your power comes not from yourself but from the connection you have and the power that moves through you. Ego disconnects you from others and God. Humility connects you. When you are humble you don't seek to gain power; you become a conduit of power for others. Imagine yourself trying to blow up a balloon. You will likely have trouble doing it with one breath. But God's power created and expanded the universe. You are one with this power, and when you let go of your ego, you become a more powerful force in this world. Here's a review of what comes from separateness and oneness.

Separateness

Oneness

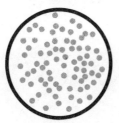 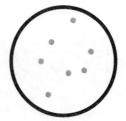

Ego	Humility
Narcissist	Integrity
Fame	Purpose
Resister	Conductor
Fear	Love
Unworthiness	Worthy
Me	We
Selfish	Selfless

Chapter 3

The Power Behind the One Truth

Connected to What?

When I recently taught the One Truth to a friend and shared some of the applications, he responded, "This is really great and helpful but one with what? Connected to what? What are we one with? What are we connected to?" In essence, he wanted to go deeper and get to the heart and power behind the One Truth. Deep down he knew there was more – and actually there is a lot more.

When I initially taught him the applications to everyday life, I didn't mention God, but when he asked what we are connected to, I had to tell him about the power behind the One Truth. I would have been doing him – and you – a disservice if I didn't talk about this power. It would be like talking about breathing and not mentioning oxygen or discussing a rocket launch without sharing the power that makes the launch possible. So I told my friend that we are connected to a higher and greater power that created us. Almost every spiritual tradition and spiritual understanding believes in a connection to the supernatural and that we are part of a greater divine creation that is more spiritual than physical in nature.

Everything Is Spiritual

Our spiritual existence makes more sense when you remember that everything you see in the world is energy. It appears physical but it's all energy. Einstein taught us that $E=mc^2$. That tree you chopped down for firewood creates heat because it's energy. The ground you are walking on feels solid but at the core it's energy vibrating slowly enough to appear solid. Your body that seems physical is made up of trillions of vibrating energy cells with atoms as the building block. And what is an atom made of but subatomic particles and mostly empty space. The foundation of our world – and us – is not physical but energetic and spiritual. Scientifically, we are more light beings than physical beings. We are not a body with a soul. We are a soul and spirit with a temporary body. Our soul carries a unique spiritual DNA and purpose, which we are meant to express on our journey through life, and along with our spirit is meant to connect to God's eternal infinite spirit.

We Were Created for Connection

Our energetic bodies turn to dust when we die, but our spirit and soul are meant to be connected to something greater than ourselves. Just as a fish is meant to live in water, and a tree is meant to be connected to the earth and soil in order to thrive, we are meant to live connected to our Creator. Because we were made for connection, we don't feel quite right when are not connected. We feel empty at times, longing for something more: searching for love and purpose, wanting to feel like we matter and are part of something greater than ourselves. So often our soul feels splintered and we know there is something missing that will fill the hole in our soul and will make us feel whole. Too often this connection feels elusive and the search feels like an imaginary quest that is a waste of time. But if we have a desire for connection, then clearly there is something we are meant to connect to. After all, if you have a desire to connect but there was nothing to connect to, then it would be futile and pointless, like trying to connect with someone who doesn't like you or want to talk to you – a big waste of time.

But that is not the case with God. God created you for connection. God wants to connect with you and put your desire for connection in your heart because you are meant to connect with the Creator of the universe. It's not futile. It's essential for your health and wholeness. I don't believe God is a religion. God is a relationship and we were created to be in relationship with our Creator and with one another. We were designed for relationships. It's why people get depressed when they are alone and isolated and why loneliness is an epidemic that is more dangerous to your health than many diseases. It's why millions of people are searching for purpose and love. We were made with love, for love, and love is the essence of who and what we are. God is love and God loves you. When you feel disconnected and separate from this source, you feel tired, fearful, hopeless, and drained. Like a tree disconnected from its soil, you wilt. Yet when you are connected to God and love, you feel plugged into the ultimate power source.

The Truth Is Simple and Powerful

I know that not everyone believes in God and that's okay. The truth doesn't need us to believe in it for it to be true. Gravity still exists whether we believe in it or not. However, the more you understand the One Truth, the more obvious it becomes that there is a greater supernatural power at work, especially when you realize that there are two main frequencies: a force that is always trying to divide you and a power that is always trying to unite you. The more you understand the force that divides and how it divides, the more obvious the existence of the power that unites becomes. The closer we get to truth, the simpler and more powerful the lesson. Humans often make things complicated, but the truth isn't complicated. The truth is that it all comes down to oneness and separateness.

In the next chapter I'm going to share a revolutionary idea that the brain is an antenna with two main frequencies that we can tune into: positive and negative. These frequencies affect the battle for our mind that I talked about in Book I. This battle is waged between the unseen forces that try to weaken and separate us and the power that wants to strengthen and unite us. Once you understand that everything in life is about oneness and separateness, then the power that is good and the forces that are evil make even more sense. Evil seeks to divide. Good unites. Once you understand good and evil, the power that heals what the forces break becomes almost undeniable. Once you understand that healing is the answer to our separation, then the ultimate solution to our ultimate separation will be obvious. In Book III I'm also going to explain how you can tap into this power and the tools you can use to avoid separation and heal your mind, body, and soul from the separation you've experienced.

BOOK
III

The Solution to
the Separation

Chapter 1

The Brain Is an Antenna

The Brain Is an Antenna

I was walking one day when a thought popped into my head that the brain is an antenna. I had been thinking about how thoughts work and trying to figure out why people with mental health issues experience more negative thoughts, separation, and depression. If thoughts are spiritual and no one has ever found them inside of a brain, then what is the relationship between brain health and mental health? Why does a healthy brain lead to more positive thoughts, whereas an unhealthy brain leads to more negative thoughts? What is the mechanism whereby thoughts and the brain interface and interconnect? Once I realized that the brain is more than just the hardware where the activation of a thought happens and that it is also an antenna that tunes into positive and negative frequencies, it all became clear.

Consider that we perceive and interact with the world through vibrations, wavelengths, frequencies, color and sound spectrums, electromagnetic fields, electrical impulses, neurosynaptic connections, neurons firing in the brain and the quantum mind and field we are just beginning to understand. Think about how we see the world. The light hits the retina and photo receptors turn the light into electrical signals that travel to the optic nerve of the brain, which then turns the signals into the images we see. Think about how we hear. Sound waves enter the outer ear and travel to the ear canal, creating vibrations, and nerve endings transform the vibrations into electrical impulses that travel to the auditory nerve to the brain, which interprets these signals. As we interact with our world, our brain – without our guidance – is constantly converting vibrations and wave lengths into electrical signals that the brain interprets to create our reality. Even at the neurological level, a synapse occurs in our brain when the axon tip of a transmitter connects to a receiver. In essence, we have little antennas in our brain that are responsible for how the brain communicates and perceives the world.

An antenna is a device designed to transmit and/or receive signals within a certain frequency range. Our brain tunes into both positive and negative frequencies, and I'm convinced that as we move from oneness to separateness we move from positive to negative because the energetic structure of our brain/antenna, tunes into a lower frequency. Negative thoughts operate at a lower frequency, whereas positive thoughts operate at a higher frequency. The more we tune into negative thoughts, such as fear, worry, doubt, jealousy, anger, or unworthiness, these thoughts negatively affect our antenna, which causes it to tune into and receive more negative thoughts. When we tune into positive thoughts such as love, hope, joy, faith, optimism, and belief, we tune into a higher frequency and nourish our brain, creating a strong and healthy antenna that tunes into more positive thoughts.

Like all things in nature, your brain is an energetic structure that is affected by the energy it receives and trans-
mits. Of course, this is an oversimplification of what's
happening, and a deeper dive into neuroscience and
conducting advanced research is necessary to explore
the process by which this happens. In studying this sub-
ject, it appears there are many theories but no definitive answers on how this all works. My theory has not
yet been tested or proven, but my hope is that scientists will consider these ideas when conducting studies
to better understand mental health and how the brain
and thoughts work. I believe they will be transformative
and lead to pioneering research, revolutionary discover-
ies, and innovative treatments to elevate our mind and
mental health. Unfortunately, most of science has yet to
make this connection, but when they do it will drive a
greater understanding and solutions for mental health
disorders.

For instance, most scientists think that coordination
of neurosynaptic connections and neurons firing are
what create thoughts, when actually it's the thoughts
that cause the neurons to fire and connect. They think
that our brains create consciousness and are looking
for consciousness within the brain, but you'll never find
consciousness in the brain, because the brain doesn't
create consciousness. It is the hardware that allows us
to experience consciousness and this reality. Our brain
doesn't create the mind. Our mind is what creates the
brain. Our soul, which includes the mind, is the software.

The brain is the hardware/antenna. Where and how our thoughts activate in our brain have an impact on the health and function of the brain. The software we run on our hardware affects the hardware, and our hardware determines the frequency it tunes into. Lower-quality software and hardware lead to separation and illness, but optimal software and hardware lead to wholeness and health.

This is why the more depressed someone is, the more negative thoughts they have, which leads to worsening depression. It's why when someone has negative thoughts, it often leads to more negative thoughts and a downward spiral. Negative thoughts affect the brain, which affects the antenna, which causes it to tune into more negative thoughts and the anxiety, fear, depression, and separation gets worse. My theory also explains the connection between drug use, chemicals, certain medications, food colorings, excessive sugar, cannabis, alcohol, and depression and mental health. When someone does drugs or eats foods that create inflammation in the brain, this damages the mitochondria (the energy factories in each cell) along with the communication pathways and the antenna, which then tunes into lower-frequency thoughts. This explains why a college student who was having tons of anxiety told me that a few days after he drinks and smokes pot on the weekend he feels depressed and alone. It explains why every mental health issue includes frequent negative thoughts. It's why mental health issues involve people feeling and acting more isolated, alone, separate, and disconnected. As they move from oneness to separateness they tune into a lower frequency and their thoughts, emotions, moods, and lives reflect this separation.

My theory also explains why certain foods like wild salmon have been shown to reduce and even eliminate depression. As you eat foods containing things like omega-3s that are responsible for providing your body with healthy fats and energy that build a healthy brain, your brain's antenna gets better and stronger and tunes into a higher frequency. It's why certain foods negatively affect our antenna as well. My son has a severe gluten allergy, and over the years I've noticed a clear pattern between him eating gluten and getting depressed. When I figured out this pattern, I reminded him often that there was nothing wrong with him. His antenna was simply temporarily damaged. When the food left his system and he went back to working out and exercising, and elevating his frequency and mind, his mindset and thoughts improved.

My theory explains why cognitive behavior therapy has been shown to be effective in improving mental health. As we have more positive thoughts and tune into a higher frequency, we take more positive actions and create an upward cycle. It's why the tips I shared in Book I on how to elevate your mind work and have a positive impact. It's why and how my walks of gratitude, prayer, trust, optimism, and belief over the years helped me overcome my depression and anxiety as I rewired my brain, and improved the quality of my antenna and the thoughts I was tuning into. As you tune into a higher frequency of love, joy, hope, faith, silence, trust, and prayer, you tap into the positive and higher frequency instead of the negative, lower frequency. This, in turn, has a huge impact on your wholeness and mental health.

You Are Part of an Epic Story

Once you understand that the brain is an antenna and everything in life comes down to oneness and separateness, then understanding the existence and battle of good and evil is essential, worthwhile, and even logical. Please stay with me as I explain the bigger story you and I are living in. You see, evil seeks to divide and good unites. You are not just living a life, you are living a story, and you are part of the epic battle between good and evil. In fact, the story plays out within you, leading to oneness or separateness. The forces that divide you and the power that unites you are at war, and your mind, body, and soul are the battleground where it all takes place. This may sound dramatic, because it is. Maybe you thought life was insignificant and your struggles were just a series of coincidental random accidents and challenges that made you feel even more insignificant. But the truth is that there's a pattern and fabric to your existence. There's wholeness and there are forces constantly trying to tear you apart and create holes that lead to every dysfunction and weakness. Evil exists in the space between humans and God. With oneness there is no space for evil to exist. But if you can be divided, then evil has space to tear you and the world apart. If you are honest, there have been many times in your life when you have felt this hole within you and have known something was missing. There were many times you felt like you were losing the battle. You may even feel that way right now. But now I'm going to share with you why you thought you were losing the battle and what you can do about it. In Book I, I shared with you the Five D's, but now I'm going to explain how evil is responsible for them and uses them to defeat us. Most of all I'm going to explain how important you truly are, and why your life, mental health, journey, and healing matter!

The Garden

You've heard the ancient story about Adam and Eve. They are hanging out with God in the Garden of Eden, just chilling and having a good time when a snake starts talking to Eve. A talking snake should have been the first indication that something might be wrong. But we know from the story that Eve doesn't leave; she stays and listens to the snake, who convinces her to eat fruit from the Tree of Knowledge of Good and Evil, the one tree that God forbade them to eat from. She gives the fruit to Adam to eat and as a result of defying God, a separation occurs between Adam and Eve and God. Note the key word here, "separation." That's what evil does. It's goal is to separate you from God and from others.

The Garden is a story about a truth that is woven into the fabric of our existence and reality. There is a God that is good who created you to be one with Him and there is evil that is always trying to divide and separate you from God and others. It's a battle that plays out everywhere, every day: on the airwaves, in the board room, in the bedroom, in locker rooms, in schools, on ballfields and playgrounds, on big and small screens, and in our minds. Think about every major epic movie. *Black Panther. Superman, Wonder Woman. Harry Potter, Star Wars,* and so on. They are all about the battle between good and evil. They resonate with us and our soul because it's the ultimate narrative in the universe and inside of us. Long before there was Luke Skywalker and Darth Vader, Batman and the Joker, there was Adam and Eve, a serpent (evil) in the Garden, and God.

Many think this is a religious story, but the Garden isn't about religion. It's about the truth. Long before Jesus walked the earth and Christianity developed, there was this ancient Jewish story that explained oneness and the perils of isolation and disconnection. From the moment God gave us free will and the power of choice, the problem existed for everyone regardless of their religion. Religious teachings simply explain the truth that exists everywhere and inside each one of us. We all know what oneness and separateness feels like. I shared many examples about how it affects us. The fact that the Garden explains the truth and separation we experience in our lives is not a coincidence. It's a part of each one of us, our story and path to move from separateness to oneness.

Truth and Lies

When I was teaching Book I to a suicidal teenager, he astutely asked me in the beginning of the teaching where negative thoughts came from if they didn't come from us. I told him, as I told you, that they come from a spiritual place. But then I explained further that there is a battle going on between good and evil. After all, why would negative thoughts exist at all if evil didn't exist? Many believe that negative thoughts are the result of evolution and developed to help us scan for danger and run from tigers and stay alive. But this theory doesn't explain the negative thoughts that attack your identity, worthiness, and purpose. Evil does this and it uses negative thoughts and the Five D's to separate you from God so you will lose the battle and be defeated.

You are a hero with a purpose and a destiny and you have an enemy whose goal is to keep you from the path, purpose, and power you are meant to experience. Your enemy plans, schemes, and lies to separate you, whereas God always wants to unite you back to Him. Your enemy's tools of choice are arrows of negative thoughts and lies that constantly target you to disorient, distract, discourage, deceive, and divide you.

The Garden gives us a great description of what happens to us. When God placed Adam and Eve in the Garden, He told them they could eat from all the trees in the Garden except one. So what did the serpent (evil) do? He got them to focus on the one tree that they couldn't eat from by lying and deceiving them. The serpent said, "Did God really say you couldn't eat from all the trees in the Garden?" No, God said they couldn't eat from the one tree, but through deception and his words he created doubt about whether God could be trusted. With this seed of doubt the serpent persuaded Adam and Eve to question their identity. He told them that if they ate from this tree they would be like God. But here's the interesting thing. Before this moment it is written in the story that they were made in the likeness and image of God, which means they already were like God. Evil lied to them and got them to forget the truth that they were like God and caused them to believe the lie that they weren't. Many say they ate of the tree out of pride because they wanted to be like God. Actually they ate the fruit because they believed the lie that they weren't. The lie led to pride, which led to the fall.

The same thing happens to us every day. This battle is still going on. We have an enemy that is constantly lying to us, causing us to forget the truth of oneness and to believe the lie that leads to further separation. The enemy will always attack you in the place of your identity and cause you to go from knowing to searching.

Instead of letting you know that you are meant to be one with God and are a child of God, the enemy will lie to you and constantly try to make you believe you aren't, which leads to separation and searching and eventually to suffering.

Yes, the enemy is always shooting arrows of lies at you, but thankfully God has given you the armor of truth to go through life victorious. You just have to receive the truth, know the truth, remember the truth, and live it. I believe I was meant to write this book to help you do just that. There is ancient Scripture that says, "Nothing can separate you from the love of God." The meaning of this is truly profound and extremely significant. This means that you are always connected to the love of God. Nothing can separate you. You are actually always one with God's love.

You either didn't know this truth or you have forgotten this truth. But now I'm telling you the truth. You are always one with God's love. And even when you know it, you need to keep reminding yourself of it, because evil does a great job of convincing you otherwise and getting you to believe the lie. How does evil do this? Let's talk about the two frequencies.

The Two Frequencies

Most of us have heard the story of the two wolves. I changed it a little bit to feature dogs so I could use it in my book *The Positive Dog*. The story is an ancient Chero-kee legend about a grandfather teaching his grandson about the battle that goes on inside of people. "My dear grandson," he says, "the battle between two 'wolves' is inside us all. One is evil. It is anger, envy, jealousy, sor-row, regret, greed, arrogance, self-pity, guilt, resentment, inferiority, lies, false pride, superiority, and ego. The other is good. It is joy, peace, love, hope, serenity, humility, kindness, benevolence, empathy, generosity, truth, com-passion, and faith." The grandson reflected for a moment and then asked his grandfather, "Which wolf wins?" The old Cherokee replied, "The one you feed."

We've also seen the image in pop culture, in movies, TV shows, and cartoons, with the devil speaking to the person over one shoulder while an angel speaks over the other shoulder. Throughout the story, the main char-acter listens to both voices and has a choice of which one to follow.

It's these same two voices that were present in the Gar-den. In fact, when Eve listens to the serpent it's the first time in the Scriptures that humans listened to another voice besides God. After they believed the lie, ate the fruit from the tree, and felt guilt and shame, they hid behind a tree. Evil loves when you hide from God because this keeps you from connecting to God. When God shows up, he calls to Adam, asking where he is. Adam replies, "I heard you in the garden and I was afraid because I was naked so I hid." God then asks, "Who told you that you were naked?"

As my friend Erwin McManus brilliantly taught me, in this instance God doesn't say, "What were you thinking, why did you do that, how could you do this?" That's what most of us would do if our kids messed up and did something they weren't supposed to do. Instead, God points directly to the main cause, and points out they were listening to a voice other than God's, and when you do this it leads to fear and separation.

Woven into an ancient Cherokee story, pop culture, psychology, and ancient biblical stories is the truth and reality of our existence. We have a choice between two voices, two frequencies: one positive and one negative. One leads to unity, wholeness, love, and positivity. The other leads to division, separation, fear, and negativity.

What Are You Tuning Into?

When listening to the radio, every radio station is simultaneously being broadcasted over the airwaves. However, you hear only the station that you tune into. In the same way, you can listen to station 1111 The Truth and tune into the faith, love, hope, belief, peace, and joy that come from God and give you life, confidence, courage, and calm. Or you can tune into AM 666 The LIE and listen to fearful words that create doubt, and discourage, distract, deceive, divide, and weaken you. God's station broadcasts messages to move you toward your destiny, while your enemy's station sends you messages that lead to your demise in an attempt to destroy God's plan for your life. Your destiny is voice activated, so what you tune into matters greatly. The frequency and words you tune into, believe, and trust will literally lead to your weakness, separation, and defeat, or to your strength, wholeness, and victory. It's a simple choice between your destruction and your destiny.

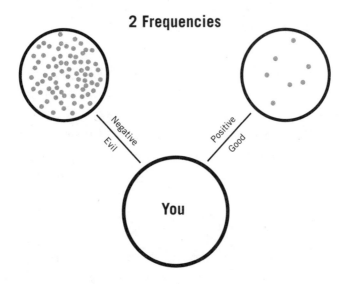

2 Frequencies

Distinguish Between Truth and Lies

One of the questions I often get is how can you tell which voice is which when you try to tune into God. The key is to know the truth so well that the lies are easy to spot. For example, counterfeit money experts don't study all types of counterfeit money. They simply study the real thing so well and know it so well that they can spot the fakes. It's why I don't believe in analyzing your negative thoughts. Since they are lies that come from a liar, why would you spend time with them? I don't spend time with liars. I hang out with the truth instead and I want to encourage you to do the same. The more you study the truth and apply it, the easier it will be to recognize the lies. And the truth is that God's truth will always speak life, hope, joy, and encouragement to you. God will always call you to more. The more you tune into Him, the simpler it will be for you to discern truth from the lies, and when you spot the lies it's easier to ignore them. At the end of the book I provide an action plan to help you TUNE into God's voice and truth.

Science Is the Search for the Truth

I realize that for some in the scientific community and those who don't believe in God, it may be strange or uncomfortable to read this explanation of the One Truth. But I believe that as truth seekers we need to look for the truth, and wherever we find it, we must share it, especially since too many are suffering with fear, anxiety, stress, depression, and mental health issues. Despite more people taking medications, more people in the world are struggling and suffering. The problem is only getting worse, not better. Anxiety is an epidemic. One of the reasons why so many in the scientific and medical community have not been able to see the truth of how the brain and thoughts work is because that would require them to see the spiritual nature of thoughts and consciousness. It would require a scientist to acknowledge the battle of good and evil that is playing out every day in our world. It would mean that you would realize our brain is an antenna and we have a choice between two frequencies. But once you understand it all comes down to the concept of oneness and separateness, and we have an antenna that tunes into either positive or negative thoughts, and brain health effects mental health, and our thoughts impact the brain, then the battle of good and evil for our mind and soul makes even more sense and the problems and solutions become obvious.

Truth is truth and you'll find it everywhere if you are looking for it. And the wild thing is that the very problems we face are detailed and explained in the Bible and the solutions are provided. Note that the Bible didn't invent this truth. Christians didn't sit around and come up with the problems and answers to the battle we face. The truth already existed within our soul and reality. The Bible just happens to contain the truth as it explains the problem and provides the solutions. I saw this very clearly when my friend Garret Kramer taught me about high and low states of mind. He is not a Christian but is a non-duality teacher. The more he explained it, the more clearly I saw how it all came down to oneness and separateness and good and evil. I explained to him that this is exactly what the Bible says. As we explored the worlds of consciousness, science, non-duality, and spirituality together, it became clear they all pointed in the same direction. When science, psychology, the Scriptures, and reality point to the same thing and it can't be refuted, you know it's the truth.

Consider that Genesis says that it's not good for humans to be alone, and science now shows us how isolation negatively affects your mental health, whereas a loving relationship helps you heal. Since I study both science and the Bible, I consistently see how science and faith overlap, and how science proves the truths in the Bible. One is the truth and one is the search for the truth, so it makes sense that the search will lead to the truth. As science evolves even further, I believe it will prove the truth found inside our souls and the Scriptures. Garret even told me recently that what he loved about reading the Bible was that it was a prescription to bring us back to oneness and provided tools for what separateness, searching, and suffering create.

Timeless Tools to Tune into the Truth

The truth is you'll never be able to win a spiritual battle with manmade solutions. And as we look at biblical teachings, it will blow your mind to see that the solutions we need to heal our mind and soul and bring us back to oneness are there waiting for us. As I mentioned earlier, the Old Testament ancient Jewish story of Adam and Eve reveals the problem of separation, and as we look at the

New Testament we find the solutions to our problem. For example, the Apostle Paul says we must take every thought captive as he explains the spiritual warfare we face when the enemy tries to fill our mind with negative thoughts. Remember, our evil enemy is a liar that is always broadcasting negative thoughts to us in order to separate us. If we don't take our thoughts captive, they will take us captive. This means tuning your radio dial to a new frequency and receiving a new station. It means replacing a negative thought with a positive thought like Dr. James Gills did, as I mentioned in Book I. In fact, Dr. James Gills would often memorize and recite Scripture, and this allowed him to take his thoughts captive. I'm pretty sure he learned it from Jesus, who taught us how to speak truth to the lies. When He was in the wilderness being tempted and lied to by the devil, He responded to every lie with the words "It is written." He said, "Man shall not live by bread alone, but by every word that proceeds from the mouth of God." He's telling us that God's words written in the Scriptures and in our hearts are bread that can nourish us, and we are meant to tune into God's words, not the lies of the enemy. Two thousand years ago we received the prescription of how to tune into the positive frequency and win our battle today.

The apostle Paul knew this battle well. As he advised in Ephesians, "To put on the full armor of God to battle evil with the belt of truth buckled around your waist, with the breastplate of righteousness, with the readiness that comes from the gospel of peace, take up the shield of faith, with which you can extinguish all the flaming arrows of the evil one, the helmet of salvation and the sword of the Spirit, which is the word of God."

Right here, Paul gives us everything we need to win the battle. Once you know how the battle is being waged and the weapons of words and thoughts your enemy uses, you can win the battle with the truth, living the right way, preparing your mind for battle, having faith, and by letting God's words and spirit live through you and guide you. When you do this, you'll be transformed by the renewing of your mind, as Paul says in Romans. In essence he's saying that by choosing what frequency we are tuning into and by connecting to God and listening to His voice and His words and being filled with His spirit, we will be transformed by the renewing of our minds. Evil tries to destroy your mind and God renews it.

Now look around and see all the people grappling with anxiety, stress, depression, fear, countless negative thought patterns, and other mental struggles. What do they need? What do you need most? A renewing of your mind, and when you do you'll be transformed. Isn't that a beautiful and wonderful image? Renew your mind and be transformed. Negative thinking will be replaced by positive thinking. Lies replaced by truth. Oneness instead of separation. The truth is in front of us. The tools are available to us, but we must make the choice to use them. Unfortunately, many don't make the choice to do good; they often make bad choices and as a result

The Brain Is an Antenna

they suffer instead. Paul said in Romans 8:5–6, "Those who live according to the flesh have their minds set on what the flesh desires; but those who live in accordance with the Spirit have their minds set on what the Spirit desires. The mind governed by the flesh is death, but the mind governed by the Spirit is life and peace." It's a clear choice between death and life. Why many don't choose the truth that gives us life and what we can do about it is what I share with you in the next chapter.

Chapter 2

The Ultimate Separation and Solution

A big part of the battle between good and evil is free will. Free will is the choice we have to tune into the positive or the negative frequency. To choose love or fear, trust or doubt, hope or despair, to use the tools God has given us to win the battle or to pretend they don't exist. Every moment of every day we can choose what is good for us or bad for us. It's like we have a piece of a fruit and a cookie sitting in front of us each morning and we get to choose what we put into our body. We know the piece of fruit is better for us and yet so often we choose the cookie. We choose what weakens us rather than what strengthens us. We choose to limit ourselves instead of living a life of unlimited possibilities. We choose to become less, not more. The big question is why do we so often choose the cookie instead? Why do we choose what gives temporary pleasure and regret, instead of long-term sustained health? When we feel separate we fill the gap with things we think will make us feel good but actually only make us feel worse. We try to fill the gap with everything but the connection to God that we truly seek. We do this because the lies of our enemy cause us to choose what is fake instead of real.

Fake and Real

One day when talking with my friend Erwin McManus, I said that I noticed that there is real and fake in all of existence. There's fake money and real money. Fake and real luxury items. Fake and real people. Fake friends and real friends. Fake food and real food from nature. Fake gods and the real God. Fake ways people seek relief but only God's love and connection gives real relief. I asked him why there is real and fake in all of existence. Is it because there are truth and lies? He responded, "It's because the evil one cannot create, he can only imitate and corrupt. Otherwise he would have created a better option than God to woo us away. Evil does not create; it corrupts. It cannot imagine, it imitates." I responded, "But even though it can't create and can only imitate, evil does a great job of lying to us and convincing us that the imitation is better or will make us feel better." And so we often go through life believing the lies and choosing the imitations instead of the real thing. We fill our separation with everything fake that leads to us continually seeking and wanting more, instead of connecting with the God who wants so much more for us and gives us everything we need to create it. These lies lead to millions choosing fake feelings of pleasure that lead to addictions that destroy lives. They want the real thing, a connection with God, but they end up choosing the imitations instead, and now you know it's because the enemy is a great deceiver, imitator, and corrupter of the truth who convinces far too many that the imitations are better.

Temptation

Temptation is the result of believing the lie, looking outside instead of inside, and being tempted to choose the imitation instead of the real thing. Temptation causes you to look away from oneness toward separateness and makes you want to choose what will further separate and divide you instead of bringing you closer to God. Temptation starts in the mind and leads you toward the sin that further separates you. Temptation is why so many who know the truth act on the lies. The enemy is so good and subversive at distorting, corrupting, and deceiving us that he convinces good people to do bad things. Yet we know temptation and sin never deliver what they promise because they are based on a lie that causes you to choose fake instead of real. In the Garden, the story said the fruit was appealing to Eve. She was tempted by it. She was told she would be like God if she ate the fruit. The lie told her she would become more if she acted on the lie, but in turning away from God and not trusting in what He said and choosing to sin, she became far less. And we do the same thing every time we are tempted and choose to believe the lie and act on the lie. Temptation leads to sin.

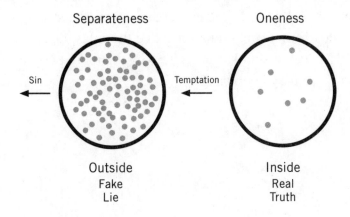

The Ultimate Separation and Solution

Sin Separates

As we discussed earlier, evil uses the Five D's to tempt and ultimately divide. In the Garden, the enemy used words and thoughts to get Adam and Eve to believe the lie and then to ultimately act on it and engage in a sinful act that led to the separation of man and woman from God and each other. If you look around, you'll see how the enemy continues to do that to us and we continue to take the bait. Anyone who has been in a marriage where one spouse cheated knows how this sin led to separation in the relationship with each other and God. It likely started as a thought of doubt and distortion, which led to discouragement and or distraction, which led to a sinful action and division. The enemy knows he can't beat us himself. So what does he do? He gets us to believe the lies one thought, one situation, one cluttered mind at a time, so that we will feel separate and eventually do things that defeat and separate ourselves. The truth is that sin doesn't make us feel good, because it separates. It doesn't feel good because it creates a wound in our soul that leads to shame, guilt, negative thoughts, depression, and a cycle of sinful actions. It's why the more people sin, the more they keep sinning.

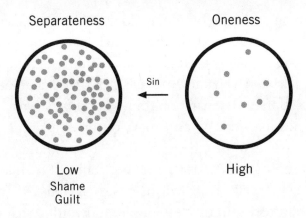

Separateness · Oneness

Sin ←

Low
Shame
Guilt

High

We usually don't like to talk about sin because we would rather keep it hidden than expose it. But I've found that the more we talk about it, the better we are able to bring it to the light and deal with it so we can heal the wounds that sin causes. What we uncover, God will cover with His grace. What we cover up will eventually be uncovered. We all have wounds. Some are caused by our own sinful actions and some are caused by the sinful actions of others. Some wounds are the result of both and we must acknowledge them as part of our healing process so we can choose oneness instead of separation. We can live with a hole inside of us or chose to become whole.

Wounds and Healing

Everyone has wounds from the past that affect our development, our brain, and our soul. The wound (trauma, painful experience, memory) causes a split in our soul and brain as we feel the pain, look at the circumstance, and become defined by the shame, pain, and guilt of it. Shame makes you want to hide. Hiding requires you to isolate and separate yourself from God and others. In isolation and separation, the wound gets worse and becomes infected. When I think of this scenario I think of the sexual abuse experienced by far too many people. It's pure evil to take away the innocence of a child and that's what evil does. Evil uses sexual abuse to make the child feel unprotected, unsafe, unworthy, shameful, and separate and disconnected from God and others. Survivors of abuse have trouble trusting and connecting because they have been betrayed by people that betrayed their trust. They feel unsafe and often anxious because they weren't protected by those they looked to for protection, God included. The lack of trust makes them want to hide even more, and the more they separate themselves, the worse they get. Think about it: the very trust and connection you need to have in order for healing to take place is sabotaged so that you'll be divided and defeated.

R. A. Dickey was a major league baseball pitcher who became a better pitcher and an all-star later in his career. I read an article about him that explained that he was a survivor of sexual abuse, which he had kept hidden most of his life and pitching career. But when he finally sought help and talked about it publicly, everything improved for him. He pitched better than ever despite being a lot older. He said, "When I stopped hiding in life, I stopped hiding on the pitching mound." It's the same for you and me. When you stop hiding, you can start healing.

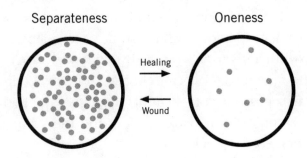

You don't have to hide when you know the truth that it's not your fault. You don't have to feel fear when you know you are truly loved. You don't have to blame yourself when you know we all have a common enemy to blame. I know abuse well and I just want you and those you know who have suffered from it to know that shame and guilt are what evil uses to create inflammation in your soul. When your body is inflamed, healing can't take place. When your brain is inflamed from a concussion or your nerve cells are inflamed from drugs or another substance, healing can't happen. Inflammation creates separation within you and prevents you from healing. The key is to remove the inflammation so you can heal.

The Ultimate Separation and Solution

In this same way, sin causes a wound in your soul, and shame and guilt represent the inflammation of the soul. But thankfully God always provides a healing solution, a way to remove this inflammation so healing can take place. Love and forgiveness are the healing mechanisms God gives us to stop blaming our past, reclaim our present, and create our future. So no matter what wound you have from your past, whether it was inflicted upon you or by you, you don't have to hide anymore. You can choose to heal. Where the wound separates you, healing through love and forgiveness unites you back to God and the connection and oneness you seek.

Love and Forgiveness

In our blame, pain, and shame we must remember the truth that God loves us and forgives us. When we receive this love and forgiveness, and love and forgive ourselves, God is able to heal us. But he doesn't just want to heal us. He wants to strengthen us and restore us to become all that we are meant to be and all that He created us to be. He wants us to live with love, power, and a high state of mind instead of fear and a low state of mind. He wants to connect with us to give us clarity, confidence, and courage. He wants to restore what has been broken and heal the hole within us and make us whole. He wants us to experience oneness, not separateness. He wants us to be joined together in one spirit. But He doesn't make us do it. He gives us a choice.

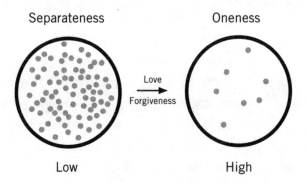

Separateness   Oneness

Love
Forgiveness

Low   High

Every day is a choice to decide between living from our wound and separation or from our healing and oneness. We can choose the fake Band-Aids that cover up the wound but don't heal it, or we can choose the real love and healing that God has given us.

Once you understand oneness and separateness and see how evil is always trying to make you sin and separate you and that there is a God who is always trying to heal and unite you back to Him through love and forgiveness, then this leads to the ultimate solution to the ultimate problem (sin and separation).

The Ultimate Solution

If the Garden represents the separation of man and woman from God, then God, who always provides a healing mechanism, would then provide a way to restore us and bring us back to Him, and thankfully He does this very thing through Jesus. In fact, if you read and learn about Jesus, His whole purpose is to make you whole. It's mind-blowing to think that the ancient Old Testament story of Adam and Eve that explains the problem of separation would be followed thousands of years later by Jesus walking the earth to provide the solution. The two stories fit together here too perfectly to be an accident. They fit because they are the truth and they perfectly explain the one truth. Remember the truth doesn't need the Bible to exist. It already exists. The Bible is what God used to explain it to us. And it says: Evil separates humans from God and Jesus restores and unites humans back to God. Evil creates the distance and Jesus is the bridge.

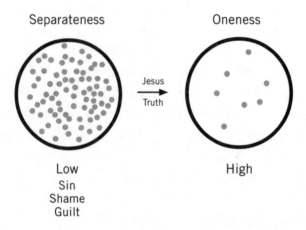

He came to take away your sin, shame, and guilt, and to dissolve your inflammation with love and forgiveness, to restore you back to wholeness and oneness. He takes your burden and your pain, saying, "Come to Me all who are weary and carry a heavy burden and I will give you rest for your soul." Evil said shame on you and Jesus said shame off you. Sin is a human problem that separates, and God knew we needed a spiritual solution to heal and become one. What happened in the Garden was reconciled on the cross. The separation and oneness are two stories that become one complete story because it's our story.

Please know that I didn't write this to convince you Jesus is the answer. I wrote it because in searching for the answer, it became clear to me that Jesus is the solution to the separation. When you understand the heart of the problem, the solution to heal the human heart and soul becomes obvious.

I've been a truth seeker my whole life. As I studied and practiced a variety of faiths and traditions, I kept searching for the truth that would explain the pain I was facing and provide the solution to this problem. As I said earlier, truth is truth and you will find it everywhere. Well, the Garden and Jesus explain the truth of oneness and separation that is happening every day within our souls, our lives, our careers, our relationships, our families, our teams, and our society. Once you see it, you can't unsee it. The problem is separation. The solution is oneness. Evil separates. Jesus unites. The Old Testament explains the problem of separation and the New Testament tells us the solutions. In it, you will find prescriptions for winning the battle of your mind, taking every thought captive, tuning into and listening to God, speaking truth to the lies, protecting yourself from the enemy's lies, and renewing your mind. It is the truth and power behind every strategy I share in Book I to win the battle of our mind and have a high state of mind.

I've shared these strategies with millions of people and they've made a huge impact, even if people didn't know the power behind them. Your soul always knows even if you don't. But when you do know and look at the big picture and see the perfect completion of the two stories and the One Truth, it's so clear that Jesus didn't just come to teach us the solution, He came to *be* the solution. He said, "I am the vine, you are the branches. If you remain in me and I in you, you will bear much fruit: apart from me you can do nothing." What is Jesus talking about here? Oneness. We have wounds through our own sins and the sins inflicted upon us. Jesus came with love and forgiveness to heal us and transform the hole in our soul to wholeness. And in wholeness you find holiness because to be whole means to be one with God and His holiness. Paul says in Corinthians, "But he who is joined to the Lord is one spirit with him." Through Jesus you become *one* spirit. God's spirit now lives in you. When you know this truth and receive it, the truth really does set you free.

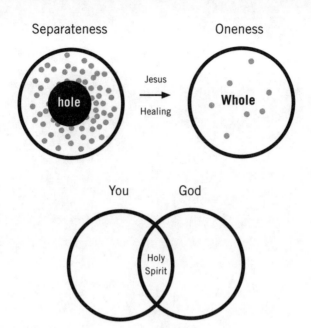

The Ultimate Separation and Solution

Chapter 3

Renewing Your Mind Forever

A Hole in the Soul

It rained a lot the other day and unfortunately we found a leak in our place. We never knew it was there because it had never rained that much. When the sun is shining and the weather is great you don't realize there are holes. But when the storms come and the rain pours down, it reveals the cracks and holes you have. If you have been through tough times in your life and are aware of the wounds you carry and have felt a hole in your soul, you know where I'm going with this.

When life is good and everything is going great, you don't think you have any issues. But when adversity strikes and the storms of life come your way, it reveals the cracks in your foundation you didn't know were there. These moments can cause you to question who you are, what you are made of, and whether you were as strong as you thought. Challenges often reveal the cracks in your identity, character, and confidence. They expose the wounds you carry and holes in your soul. During these times, you can allow the revelation of these cracks to break you or cause you to seek ways to break through. You can believe storms are happening to you or for you. You can allow adversity to weaken you and crush your identity or find ways to reinforce your core and become even stronger. Finding holes may be difficult and inconvenient, and may cause a lot of temporary pain and frustration, but they are also great opportunities to fix what is broken, heal the wounds, fill the holes, and become whole. This is what happened to me.

As I said, I didn't write this book to convince you to believe in Jesus. I wrote it because I knew I was meant to share the One Truth and the Ultimate Truth with you. When I saw it so clearly and grasped how the understanding of oneness and separateness has helped others in a short period of time, I knew I needed to share it. Everyone is on their own journey. I never thought I would believe what I believed. I didn't know much about Jesus until I was 34 years old. I struggled with depression, anxiety, fear, and a lot of pain from my past. The cracks in my foundation made me seek ways to restore and heal myself. I found positive psychology and as I mentioned in the introduction, I began taking walks of gratitude, which eventually turned into walks of prayer. Every day I was talking to myself and talking to God and tuning into a higher frequency. I didn't know it at the time, of course, but it's clear to me now what was happening. I was improving mentally but still didn't feel peace. A friend of mine gave me some sermons from Erwin McManus; one was called "Why Jesus?" It really spoke to me, and for the first time I thought, maybe there is something to this Jesus.

I went to see a Buddhist energy healer because I was having a lot of stomach problems. I told him I was seeing signs on the road a lot that said Jesus is the answer.

He proceeded to tell me that Jesus takes our soul pain; Christians call it sin. He said I wouldn't be able to connect with God if I carried this heavy vibrational energy. I asked if I could remove someone else's soul pain, sin, and heavy energy. He asked, "Can you handle your own?" He was showing me the hole in my soul. He said that as a Buddhist, he was trying to obtain enlightenment on his own. But with Jesus all you do is believe and receive. I walked out of there believing there was a God who would want to heal me and take my burden and pain. This belief changed my life.

The Vine and the Branch

I decided to follow Jesus because I knew my soul needed healing and saving and I couldn't save myself, and everything changed. I practiced everything I wrote about in this book. I read, I prayed, I practiced gratitude, I trusted, I surrendered often, and I kept connecting with God and letting God connect with me. I became a better husband and father. My depression went away. I realized my mind needed renewing and my soul needed healing. As I renewed my mind and healed my soul, I experienced more oneness, which caused me to tune into more positive thoughts, love, hope, and peace that over time nourished and renewed my mind and brain. I felt a greater intimacy and personal connection with God and over time His purpose and wisdom started to flow through me. Friends will tell you that I'm actually smarter than I was and have so many more great ideas and much more wisdom, and I know without a doubt that it's not coming from me. The One Truth and this book certainly didn't come from me. The 27 books I've written before this one didn't come from me. I've made it a practice to surrender and trust and let the Holy Spirit live in me and through me. When I do, I'm at my best. When I don't, I'm at my worst.

Am I perfect? Not at all. Do I fall short? You bet. I'm human so I still experience separation and sin, but when it happens I know how and why it's happening. I know the truth, and in reminding myself of the truth, I'm better able to take on the evil that comes my way. With that said, I know some might ask if Jesus and the New Testament are the solutions and keys to healing, then why do so many Christians still struggle with mental health and depression? The answer is because sin and evil still exist. For this reason it doesn't mean that if you believe in Jesus your life becomes perfect and you enjoy great health and become successful. Many who follow Jesus tune into fear and a negative frequency. Many have antennas that are so badly damaged that they are unable to tune into God. They experience a lot of static or the messages they receive are distorted. Many have sins that have been forgiven but they still must live with the consequences of the sin. We live in a world where evil, sin, struggle, and strife exist, and our lives and society will reflect this. Many go to church but don't live the teachings Jesus shared. They have religion but don't have a relationship. They are not united in spirit. Many know the truth, but they forget the truth and/or don't live the truth. Some have been saved but haven't taken the steps to renew their mind and heal their soul, body, and brain from the patterns and consequences of their past negative thoughts and actions. You can go to the gym or watch the workout video, but you have to do the work. Healing often takes time.

The One Truth is not about living a perfect life. It's about living a hopeful, faithful, and fruitful life. In John 15, Jesus says the word "remain" 11 times. He is saying we must remain in Him in order to be connected to Him. "If you remain in me and I in you, you will bear much fruit. Apart from me you can do nothing." The more we remain and connect with the Creator of the universe, the stronger the signal and our antenna become. This means we must make time each day to connect with God and allow His Spirit to renew our soul and mind and let healing take place.

Renewing Your Mind

We know that we heal through connection and a loving relationship. We don't heal through a relationship with a stranger. To develop a relationship with someone, you must spend time with them. If you don't spend time with your spouse, you won't have a great relationship. The same goes for God. If you don't spend time with God, you won't have much of a relationship. God will be a stranger. You must make time for the One who loves you most and created you to be loved and to love. It's essential you make the time to tune out the distractions, be still and pray, surrender, trust, read, and allow His Spirit to live in you and let His voice guide you. Positive change doesn't happen overnight. You may have been tuned in to a lower frequency for a long time. You may have a lot of bad habits. You might have a wound of pain and shame that's been infecting your soul and life for a long time. You might have had a traumatic brain injury in the past. Just as it takes a year to work out to transform your body and about eight months to heal your gut lining if you have gut health issues, it takes time for healing to take place in your brain. Renewing your mind doesn't happen instantaneously. You might make the decision to let Jesus save and heal you, but it often takes time for the healing to happen. Many will notice an immediate shift and feeling of freedom and hopefulness, yet renewing takes time.

The soul is the integrator between the flesh and the spirit that are at odds with each other. If the soul and mind are driven by the flesh, it leads to dysfunction and damage of the mind, soul, brain, and body. If the soul and mind are healed by the Spirit, it leads to a healthy mind, soul, body, and life. Baptism is the immersion of the soul in the Holy Spirit. It's not meant to be a one-time event. That would be like dunking a cucumber in pickle juice one time and expecting complete transformation to happen immediately. The cucumber must bathe in the pickle juice for a long period of time to be transformed and pickled. In this same way you will want to continuously immerse your mind and soul in the Holy Spirit to be renewed, healed, and transformed. I share more about this in the action plan at the end of this chapter.

As you make time to heal, imagine yourself each day turning that radio dial from negative to positive and connecting more with God and you'll see how His frequency raises your frequency. Over time, as the signal gets stronger, you'll experience less clutter and more peace, calm, joy, love, hope, faith, confidence, and courage. Imagine yourself choosing love instead of fear each day. See yourself healing the wounds of your past and creating your life and your future. Watch as the Holy Spirit lives in you and over time renews your mind and transforms your heart and soul. Your life won't be perfect, but you will have more peace and hope, will feel more love and connection, and will be better equipped to handle and overcome the challenges you face. It's a choice you get to make in every moment of the day: Stay separate and wither, or remain in oneness and produce more fruit in your own life and in the lives of others.

You are not meant to go through life feeling anxious, insecure, cluttered, chronically stressed, worried, and sad most of the time. You are meant to be whole and live with hope, clarity, confidence, and power to impact this world.

Forever Is Now

At some point in your life you may have asked why does any of this matter? And why do you even matter? If you are eventually going to die, why does your life matter? You could say to impact your family, your kids, others around you, and the world, but everyone you impact will die as well. Their kids and families and future generations will all die too. If we are all going to die, what's the point? Why do we make great wine if we are just going to drink it? Why do we make a great meal if we are just going to eat it? Why do we paint if the painting may end up in a basement one day? Why do we write books that may not be read in 100 years? Why do we care about winning a sports competition if no one will care or remember our name 200 years from now? Why do we care about delivering a great musical performance? Why do we care about building a company that may not be around in the future? Why do we care about being our best? Why do we care if life is temporary for all of us?

I believe we care because appearance is temporary but essence is eternal. Our bodies are temporary but our souls are eternal. This energetic reality we experience is an expression of our eternal essence. You exist both eternally and in the present moment. In fact, each present moment is an eternal moment. The love, care, and essence you put into your life, creations, and this world are an expression of the eternal soul within you. Everything you create comes from the eternal essence and so there is an eternal nature to everything that appears temporary. That amazing meal your grandmother made with love is gone, but the essence she made it with exists forever. The love and care that you put into everything are what lasts and matters. What you create matters far less than the love and essence you put into it and the character you develop and who you become while creating it.

Everything Matters and You Matter

Our lives and our oneness with God is the intersection between the temporary and the eternal, the physical and the spiritual. Everything matters because there is an eternal nature to everything that appears temporary. You matter because your eternal soul matters. While you are here on earth your soul is living in a temporary body while also existing eternally. And this is why healing your soul matters. The pain you experience in your lifetime is temporary, but the healing of your soul is eternal.

This eternal existence is the Kingdom that Jesus talked about. He said the Kingdom of God is inside of you. He talked about making earth like heaven and bringing heaven to earth. He was telling us it's all connected. It's all *one*. To be united with God in spirit is eternal life because you're eternally united with God. We aren't supposed to wait to get to heaven. We are supposed to unite with God and bring heaven here, right now. When we love, feel joy, practice gratitude, and serve others, we make Earth like Heaven. When we heal, we are able to heal others and make Earth like Heaven. Since the Kingdom is inside each person, when you impact a person's life in a loving way, you are impacting the Kingdom. We desire to impact the Kingdom and experience Heaven because our soul knows it's the purest expression of who we are. When we die and our bodies fade away, this is when we experience the purest expression of oneness, and until then we are always seeking the Kingdom and longing for Heaven. It's why we love movies filled with imaginary worlds, superheroes with supernatural powers, and mystical realities. We get a glimpse of it in beautiful sunrises and sunsets and feel a shift in our soul when we experience the love and kindness of a stranger or hear a baby laugh, swim in the ocean, or experience the zone while performing. The separation fades away and we feel the Oneness with God and the Kingdom all around us and within us. Your soul knows you are *one* and hopefully now you know it too. When you seek the Kingdom you'll find it within you and in others and when you love and heal you make Earth like Heaven and create the life and world God gave you the power to create.

You are Soul.

You are Spirit.

You are Love.

You are Whole.

You are One.

Action Plan

Full Circle

In the introduction I shared the quest I've been on my entire life to be mentally tough, improve my mindset, get better, and help others get better. As I've taught the One Truth to various people, they always ask what they should do next, what actions they can take. To help you take action and live the One Truth, I've created three acronyms that encompass the ideas, lessons, and truths from Books I, II, and III. The greatest gap in the world is the gap between knowing and doing. You may know, but you must do. So now that you know the One Truth, here is a framework to live it powerfully with simple action steps that will TUNE your dial, help you become WHOLE, and elevate your mind and soul with PRAYER.

TUNE

T: Trust and Truth

Trusting God and speaking truth begin the process of tuning to a higher frequency. In every moment you have the opportunity to believe the lie of fear and doubt, or trust in the Creator of the universe. Take time each day and talk to God and let Him know that you trust Him and His plan for your life. Whenever you start to feel fearful or have doubt, simply pause and say, "I trust in You, God." It's also very helpful to read God's truth. When you read the Bible and devotionals, you will understand the truth and the promises God made to humanity, including you. The more you know those promises, believe they will come to pass, trust in these truths, and speak truth to the lies as we discussed in the book, the more you raise your frequency.

U: Unite with God

To unite with God you must make time to spend with God. Make time each day for prayer where you practice gratitude, praise God, repent to God, surrender to God, trust in God, and receive God and all He has for you. I usually do this on a walk and will start with gratitude, where I thank God for everything in my life, even the challenges. Then I will praise God and tell Him how awesome He is and be in awe of the universe and all of creation. Then I repent to God for not loving and trusting Him with all my heart and for falling short in other areas of my life. Then I ask God for guidance and wisdom and to provide for my needs. I surrender and ask God to make me an instrument of His peace, joy, love, and miracles He wants to see in the world. I say use me for Your purpose and guide me toward my purpose. Have me help who You want me to help and do what You want me to do. I surrender and acknowledge my need for His presence and power in my life and how I am nothing without Him. I then expect and trust God will answer my prayers and trust in His plan for my life. I trust and expect He will give me what I need and ignore what is not meant for me. Finally I receive all the love, joy, peace, and blessings God has for me, including those I am meant to help and serve. I say it out loud and receive all of God's goodness and blessings. This practice has changed my heart, soul, and life in amazing ways. I share more about this at the end of this section, where I teach a powerful way to pray using the PRAYER acronym.

N: Neutralize the Negativity

Even when you make time for God and unite with God, negativity is going to come in during the course of your day. As we discussed earlier in the book, the negativity can turn your dial to a lower frequency if you let it and can sabotage you. The key is to speak truth to the lies and positive words to the negativity when it does. On the left side of a piece of paper, write down the common negative thoughts that usually pop into your head.

151

Action Plan

On the right side of the paper, write down the words of truth and encouragement you will say to neutralize the negativity and fuel your mind with positivity. I mentioned in Book I that Dr. James Gills talks to himself instead of listening to himself, and you can do this as well any time negative thoughts come your way.

E: Elevate Your Thinking

Everything I mentioned in TUNE elevates your thinking. The key is to keep doing it. Take every thought captive. Be intentional with your thinking. Constantly return to the truth when the lies start to take hold. When you start to feel entitled or complacent, focus on appreciation. When you appreciate, you elevate. When you feel fear, remind yourself that love casts out fear and focus on loving the process rather than worrying about the outcome. When you feel lost, pray for guidance. When you feel weak, pray for strength. When you want to give up, remind yourself how far you have come and where you are going and why you are going there. When you are facing a challenge, find the opportunity to learn and grow. When you are going through a difficult time, tell yourself to stay on the roller coaster and trust that the adversity will build your character and strength. Find meaning in the mundane, purpose in the pain, and focus from the frustration. Through all your daily challenges keep thinking with faith and hope. Faith in God and hope for the future give you power in the present. Stay positive. Be optimistic. Keep believing and trusting that the best is yet to come. When you elevate your thinking, you elevate your soul and your life.

Action Plan

WHOLE

W: Walk with God

Becoming WHOLE begins with walking with the God who created you to be whole. Life is a journey; imagine you and God walking side by side in a loving and supportive relationship. As you walk with God and TUNE into Him through trust, prayer, surrender, and gratitude, you will unite with Him, feel his presence in your life, hear his voice, and receive His love and guidance. The more you walk and TUNE, the more powerful and intimate the relationship becomes.

H: Heal

As you walk with Jesus, He will reveal your wounds so they can be healed. This is often painful at first because an open wound is meant to be painful. It's a signal letting you know that it needs to be healed. If you broke your arm and didn't feel pain, you wouldn't know it needed to be reset so it can heal. Pain is a gift letting you know it needs attention so you can address it. Too often we ignore the pain, but when you walk with God He won't let you ignore it anymore. It's why many are scared to walk with God because the wound becomes exposed and the pain grows, and no one likes to feel this way. Humans spend billions of dollars to avoid or mask the pain they feel. Too many see God as the source of the pain, but as you walk with God you will realize He's only revealing the wound and allowing you to feel pain so you can heal it to become all He created you to be. Pain is temporary but Healing is eternal. God loves you and wants to heal you. You are meant to heal your wounds in order to become whole.

O: Oneness

As you walk with Jesus and heal the hole in your soul, and heal the wounds with love and forgiveness, you become One with God. As the Apostle Paul says, "We become One spirit with Him." In Oneness you experience connection, power, peace, joy, hope, faith, confidence, courage, and calm. Oneness is God's intention for us. The separation happened and He created a way to restore us, redeem us, and make us Whole in Him. As you walk with Him and TUNE into Him and Unite with Him, you Heal and become One with Him. This is not simply a religious path; it's a spiritual path between the Creator and His creation. When you walk, accept, believe, and receive, you experience the power and love that come from Oneness.

L: Love

From Oneness, love flows. God is love, so when you walk with God and heal and become one, God's love becomes your love and flows through you to others. This love transforms your heart, mind, and soul and it changes the way you see and interact with the world. Instead of looking for love, you become a source of love. And as you share this love with others, your relationships improve, your influence grows, and your power increases. Fear has no power over you when love is moving through you. The essence of the Creator is love. The driving intention of the Creator for us is a loving relationship with Him. As we walk with God and heal and develop an intimate relationship, we experience the power and presence of His love. In this Oneness, His essence becomes our essence and this elevates our thoughts, words, spirit, and actions.

E: Elevate Your Mind

If you have ever been in love, you know it feels like you are walking on air. You feel alive and elevated. That's because love is the highest frequency there is and it elevates everything about you, including your thinking, your soul, your mind, your mood, your energy, and your actions. As you walk with God, heal, and become one, love flows through you, and this renews and elevates your mind. Like a flowing river clearing out debris in its path, this renewing spirit washes away all the mud in your mind, leading to a greater connection and enhanced insights, clarity, confidence, courage, creativity, power, and peace. To bring this book full circle, when you are WHOLE you live more frequently with a higher state of mind. Your circumstances no longer have the power to transform you. You have the power to transform your circumstances from the inside out.

PRAYER

Many have shared with me that they don't know how to unite with God and they don't know how to pray. When you realize you are spirit with a soul and a fleshly body that turns to dust when you die, it makes more sense that the key to uniting with God is to unite your spirit with God's Spirit. Just as a river flows into a larger body of water and becomes one, when your spirit unites with God, you become one. When your soul bathes in this oneness, it is renewed and allows for healing to take place. If you plunge a cucumber into a large jar of pickle juice, dunking it once for a short period of time won't do much. But if that cucumber is submerged in the pickle juice for an extended period of time it becomes pickled. It gets transformed. The longer your mind/soul bathes in the Holy Spirit, the more it is renewed and healed, and then a healed mind/soul heals you at many levels of your being. Prayer is a powerful way to bathe your mind/soul in the Spirit. So let's talk about how to do that.

P: Praise

When Jesus taught us how to pray he started with "Our father, who art in heaven, hallowed be thy name." Prayer starts with praising God, worshiping and adoring Him, and being in awe of the Creator who created you and everything in existence. When you look at the One who makes the stars shine and created blue skies and oceans, sunsets and sunrises, majestic mountains and tiny mole hills, and the hundreds of trillions of cells in our bodies that allow us to experience life, God deserves our admiration. When you praise God you can also thank Him for everything in your life, big and small, you can thank Him for it all.

R: Repent

Holding on to shame, guilt, bitterness, resentment, and regret creates sludge in your pipeline that makes it hard to unite with God. A big part of prayer is to repent for the things you have done wrong and the stuff you are holding on to and ask for forgiveness in order to release it and let it go. When Jesus said to pray, "Forgive us for our trespasses as we forgive those who trespass against us," He was telling us to ask God to forgive us and to forgive others. When I repent, I ask God to forgive me for not loving and trusting Him with all my heart and to forgive me for all the wrongs I have done and forgive others who have wronged me. When you and I do this, we remove the blockages that keep us disconnected from God.

A: Ask

Now that the sludge is cleared from the pipeline and pathway to God, it's time to ask God to provide for your daily needs and to give you guidance and wisdom. I will often ask God to show me signs of where I'm supposed to go and what I'm supposed to do. I ask God to guide me in the right direction and show me the way. I ask God to protect my family and to heal us. Depending on what's going on in my life, I will ask God specifically for a solution or resolution but with the knowing and trusting that His will and plan is always best.

Y: Yield

After you ask God for what you need and for what He wants for you, it's essential to yield and surrender to God. Acknowledge your need for His presence and power in your life and let Him know you are nothing without Him. All that you are and have is because of the God that created you. Let go of your EGO that edges God out. Let go of your pride. Let go of your protective shell that keeps you separated from God. Stand before God, open your arms, and say, "I need You, God. I can't do this alone. My will isn't strong enough. I'm not powerful enough. I need Your strength. I need Your guidance. I need Your love. I surrender to You and ask that You live through me with Your love, power, and strength. Use me for Your purpose, God, and guide me toward my purpose. Make me a conduit for all that You want to do in this world through me. Have me be what You want me to be and do what You want me to do. I surrender to Your will and plan for me. Use me to build Your Kingdom, not my kingdom."

E: Expect

After you ask God and yield to God, a key part of praying that a lot of people don't talk about is to expect God to deliver. Many people pray but they don't really trust that God will answer their prayer. As a result, their prayers are weak and lack faith and conviction. When I pray, I trust and expect that God will answer my prayers. I have childlike faith and expect that He will show up in my life like a good father and provide for me. I trust in His plan for my life. I trust and expect He will give me what I need and ignore what is not meant for me. This means that while you may ask God for something, He may not deliver it right now, or ever. But you can trust that God will give you what you need in His time and the right time for you. God will open every door you are meant to walk through. I truly believe that God wants you to trust Him. He wants to show you He is real. He wants you to live an abundant life in Him. He wants you to live with His power. When you praise, repent, ask, yield, expect, and trust then you create a connection and relationship with God that enables Him to heal you, bless you, and use you for a greater purpose.

R: Receive

While a lot of people pray, they either don't trust God to deliver or they don't receive what God wants to deliver. Many pray but they don't feel worthy to receive what God wants to give them. A big part of PRAYER is to receive all that God wants to give you. You asked for it, so now expect it and receive it. When I pray, I say out loud to God, "I receive all the love, joy, peace, abundance, and blessings you have for me. I receive all the clients and people who want to work with me and all those I am meant to help and serve." I say it out loud and receive all of God's goodness and blessings. I trust and believe and receive. I want to encourage you to allow God to give you the abundance, healing, and power He wants to give you. Receive it willingly and openly. Let God bless you so you can be a blessing to others. God doesn't just want to bless you. He wants to bless through you. With your humility and His grace and the power of PRAYER, God will give you the power to be a force for good in this world.

Other Books by Jon Gordon

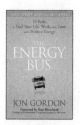

The Energy Bus

A man whose life and career are in shambles learns from a unique bus driver and set of passengers how to overcome adversity. Enjoy an enlightening ride of positive energy that is improving the way leaders lead, employees work, and teams function.

www.TheEnergyBus.com

The No Complaining Rule

Follow a vice president of human resources who must save herself and her company from ruin and discover proven principles and an actionable plan to win the battle against individual and organizational negativity.

www.NoComplainingRule.com

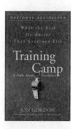

Training Camp

This inspirational story about a small guy with a big heart, and a special coach who guides him on a quest for excellence, reveals the 11 winning habits that separate the best individuals and teams from the rest.

www.TrainingCamp11.com

The Shark and the Goldfish

Delightfully illustrated, this quick read is packed with tips and strategies on how to respond to challenges beyond your control in order to thrive during waves of change.

www.SharkandGoldfish.com

Soup

The newly appointed CEO of a popular soup company is brought in to reinvigorate the brand and bring success back to a company that has fallen on hard times. Through her journey, discover the key ingredients to unite, engage, and inspire teams to create a culture of greatness.

www.Soup11.com

The Seed

Go on a quest for the meaning and passion behind work with Josh, an up-and-comer at his company who is disenchanted with his job. Through Josh's cross-country journey, you'll find surprising new sources of wisdom and inspiration in your own business and life.

www.Seed11.com

One Word

One Word is a simple concept that delivers powerful life change! This quick read will inspire you to simplify your life and work by focusing on just one word for this year. *One Word* creates clarity, power, passion, and life-change. When you find your word, live it, and share it, your life will become more rewarding and exciting than ever.

www.getoneword.com

The Positive Dog

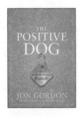

We all have two dogs inside of us. One dog is positive, happy, optimistic, and hopeful. The other dog is negative, mad, pessimistic, and fearful. These two dogs often fight inside us, but guess who wins? The one you feed the most. *The Positive Dog* is an inspiring story that not only reveals the strategies and benefits of being positive, but also an essential truth: being positive doesn't just make you better; it makes everyone around you better.

www.feedthepositivedog.com

The Carpenter

The Carpenter is Jon Gordon's most inspiring book yet—filled with powerful lessons and success strategies. Michael wakes up in the hospital with a bandage on his head and fear in his heart after collapsing during a morning jog. When Michael finds out the man who saved his life is a carpenter, he visits him and quickly learns that he is more than just a carpenter; he is also a builder of lives, careers, people, and teams. In this journey, you will learn timeless principles to help you stand out, excel, and make an impact on people and the world.

www.carpenter11.com

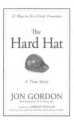

The Hard Hat

A true story about Cornell lacrosse player George Boiardi, *The Hard Hat* is an unforgettable book about a selfless, loyal, joyful, hard-working, competitive, and compassionate leader and teammate, the impact he had on his team and program, and the lessons we can learn from him. This inspirational story will teach you how to build a great team and be the best teammate you can be.

www.hardhat21.com

You Win in the Locker Room First

Based on the extraordinary experiences of NFL Coach Mike Smith and leadership expert Jon Gordon, *You Win in the Locker Room First* offers a rare, behind-the-scenes look at one of the most pressure-packed leadership jobs on the planet, and what leaders can learn from these experiences in order to build their own winning teams.

www.wininthelockerroom.com

Life Word

Life Word reveals a simple, powerful tool to help you identify the word that will inspire you to live your best life while leaving your greatest legacy. In the process, you'll discover your why, which will help show you how to live with a renewed sense of power, purpose, and passion.

www.getoneword.com/lifeword

Other Books by Jon Gordon

The Power of Positive Leadership

The Power of Positive Leadership is your personal coach for becoming the leader your people deserve. Jon Gordon gathers insights from his bestselling fables to bring you the definitive guide to positive leadership. Difficult times call for leaders who are up to the challenge. Results are the by-product of your culture, teamwork, vision, talent, innovation, execution, and commitment. This book shows you how to bring it all together to become a powerfully positive leader.

www.powerofpositiveleadership.com

The Power of a Positive Team

In *The Power of a Positive Team*, Jon Gordon draws on his unique team-building experience, as well as conversations with some of the greatest teams in history, to provide an essential framework of proven practices to empower teams to work together more effectively and achieve superior results.

www.PowerOfAPositiveTeam.com

The Coffee Bean

From bestselling author Jon Gordon and rising star Damon West comes *The Coffee Bean*: an illustrated fable that teaches readers how to transform their environment, overcome challenges, and create positive change.

www.coffeebeanbook.com

Stay Positive

Fuel yourself and others with positive energy—inspirational quotes and encouraging messages to live by from bestselling author, Jon Gordon. Keep this little book by your side, read from it each day, and feed your mind, body, and soul with the power of positivity.

www.StayPositiveBook.com

The Garden

The Garden is an enlightening and encouraging fable that helps readers overcome the 5 D's (doubt, distortion, discouragement, distractions, and division) in order to find more peace, focus, connection, and happiness. Jon tells a story of teenage twins who, through the help of a neighbor and his special garden, find ancient wisdom, life-changing lessons, and practical strategies to overcome the fear, anxiety, and stress in their lives.

www.readthegarden.com

Relationship Grit

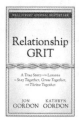

Bestselling author Jon Gordon is back with another life-affirming book. This time, he teams up with Kathryn Gordon, his wife of 23 years, for a look at what it takes to build strong relationships. In *Relationship Grit*, the Gordons reveal what brought them together, what kept them together through difficult times, and what continues to sustain their love and passion for one another to this day.

www.relationshipgritbook.com

Stick Together

From bestselling author Jon Gordon and coauthor Kate Leavell, *Stick Together* delivers a crucial message about the power of belief, ownership, connection, love, inclusion, consistency, and hope. The authors guide individuals and teams on an inspiring journey to show them how to persevere through challenges, overcome obstacles, and create success together.

www.sticktogetherbook.com

Row the Boat

In *Row the Boat*, Minnesota Golden Gophers Head Coach P.J. Fleck and bestselling author Jon Gordon deliver an inspiring message about what you can achieve when you approach life with a never-give-up philosophy. The book shows you how to choose enthusiasm and optimism as your guiding lights instead of being defined by circumstances and events outside of your control.

www.rowtheboatbook.com

The Sale

In *The Sale*, bestselling author Jon Gordon and rising star Alex Demczak deliver an invaluable lesson about what matters most in life and work and how to achieve it. The book teaches four lessons about integrity in order to create lasting success.

www.thesalebook.com

The One Word Journal

In *The One Word Journal*, bestselling authors Jon Gordon, Dan Britton, and Jimmy Page deliver a powerful new approach to simplifying and transforming your life and business. You'll learn how to access the core of your intention every week of the year as you explore 52 weekly lessons, principles, and wins that unleash the power of your One Word.

How to Be a Coffee Bean

In *How to Be a Coffee Bean*, bestselling coauthors of *The Coffee Bean*, Jon Gordon and Damon West, present 111 simple and effective strategies to help you lead a coffee bean lifestyle—one full of healthy habits, encouragement, and genuine happiness. From athletes to students and executives, countless individuals have been inspired by *The Coffee Bean* message. Now, *How to Be a Coffee Bean* teaches you how to put *The Coffee Bean* philosophy into action to help you create real and lasting change in your life.

The Energy Bus for Kids

The illustrated children's adaptation of the bestselling book, *The Energy Bus* tells the story of George, who, with the help of his school bus driver, Joy, learns that if he believes in himself, he'll find the strength to overcome any challenge. His journey teaches kids how to overcome negativity, bullies, and everyday challenges to be their best.

www.EnergyBusKids.com

Thank You and Good Night

Thank You and Good Night is a beautifully illustrated book that shares the heart of gratitude. Jon Gordon takes a little boy and girl on a fun-filled journey from one perfect moonlit night to the next. During their adventurous days and nights, the children explore the people, places, and things they are thankful for.

The Hard Hat for Kids

The Hard Hat for Kids is an illustrated guide to teamwork. Adapted from the bestseller *The Hard Hat*, this uplifting story presents practical insights and life-changing lessons that are immediately applicable to everyday situations, giving kids—and adults—a new outlook on cooperation, friendship, and the selfless nature of true teamwork.

www.HardHatforKids.com

One Word for Kids

If you could choose only one word to help you have your best year ever, what would it be? *Love? Fun? Believe? Brave?* It's probably different for each person. How you find your word is just as important as the word itself. And once you know your word, what do you do with it? In *One Word for Kids,* bestselling author Jon Gordon—along with coauthors Dan Britton and Jimmy Page—asks these questions to children and adults of all ages, teaching an important life lesson in the process.

www.getoneword.com/kids

Other Books by Jon Gordon

The Coffee Bean for Kids

From the bestselling authors of *The Coffee Bean*, inspire and encourage children with this transformative tale of personal strength. Perfect for parents, teachers, and children who wish to overcome negativity and challenging situations, *The Coffee Bean for Kids* teaches readers about the potential that each one of us has to lead, influence, and make a positive impact on others and the world.

www.coffeebeankidsbook.com

168

Other Books by Jon Gordon